Aesthetics of Pop Music

Theory Redux
Series editor: Laurent de Sutter

Aesthetics of Pop Music

Diedrich Diederichsen

Translated by George Robarts

polity

First published in 2023 by Polity Press

Polity Press
65 Bridge Street
Cambridge CB2 1UR, UK

Polity Press
111 River Street
Hoboken, NJ 07030, USA

ISBN-13: 978-1-5095-5202-3
ISBN-13: 978-1-5095-5203-0(pb)

A catalogue record for this book is available from the British Library.

Library of Congress Control Number: 2022952031

Typeset in 12.5 on 15pt Adobe Garamond
by Cheshire Typesetting Ltd, Cuddington, Cheshire
Printed and bound in Great Britain by CPI Group (UK) Ltd, Croydon

The publisher has used its best endeavours to ensure that the URLs for external websites referred to in this book are correct and active at the time of going to press. However, the publisher has no responsibility for the websites and can make no guarantee that a site will remain live or that the content is or will remain appropriate.

Every effort has been made to trace all copyright holders, but if any have been overlooked the publisher will be pleased to include any necessary credits in any subsequent reprint or edition.

For further information on Polity, visit our website:
politybooks.com

Contents

Preface

I have opted for the term 'pop music' (not pop, not rock, not R&B) because it has the widest possible scope. What I will discuss in the following chapters is as applicable to Britney Spears as it is to John Zorn, encompassing styles complex and simple, sophisticated and unsophisticated, and covering a historical period of around 65–70 years. As such, I cannot and will not go into the specific details of this corpus (beyond giving examples), but will attempt instead to pin down a general conception of pop music, proposing the contents to a theory rather than expounding the theory in full; in two far more extensive books published in German – *Über Pop Musik* [*On Pop Music*] (2014) and *Körpertreffer* [*Body*

Hits] (2017) – I have begun to attempt the latter.

Though my intellectual background is varied, I am influenced by the critical theory of the Frankfurt School – although I do not by any means share its scepticism and its judgements, perhaps even its resentments towards the cultural phenomena explored here. I shall also draw on the methodology of an old adversary of the Frankfurt School: so-called German media theory (*Medienwissenschaften*), as formulated by Friedrich Kittler. Although I disagree with some of its historical and intellectual foundations (Heidegger), I ascribe considerable importance to the construction of cultural regimes and systems by media technology. As you will see, I also take inspiration from other notable theoretical approaches (Luhmann's systems theory, Hall's cultural studies). My books, however, are not primarily academic by nature. They tend to combine the genres of the discursive text and the manifesto.

Pop Music Is a Form of Indexical Art

Hey, Bo Diddley!

The *aesthetics* of pop music, not its sociology, not its history! What is stimulating and attractive about pop music, what desires does it elicit or even satisfy, what does it instigate? Does it cause experiences of a specific nature (aesthetic experiences), and who does what kind of business with these experiences? Is business limiting the possibility of experiences? And first and foremost: is this not part of an aesthetics of music? No, on the contrary: pop music is only partly music. In fact, I shall attempt to define pop music as an entity constituted by very specific peculiarities that – across the unimaginable volume of productions, names, anecdotes, stylistic concepts and life stories that positivist pop-geek scholarship has engaged with to date – exhibit a certain consistency. Pop music always involves a musical recording, but it is also fundamentally reliant on visual images in various media and outlets; on performances connected to the recordings; on a non-teleological, more African- than European-influenced form of music; on the veneration of the star performer's body; and on the direct physical presence of the (human) voice and of (specific mechanical or electronic) sound effects, which are transmitted via indexical signals and which can be recognized in public and live settings, whereby the recipients are activated in a certain way. These aesthetic qualities demand a different approach from that of theories and histories of pop music focused principally on sociology/ethnography or musicology – not to mention the countless autobiographies penned by musicians and fans.

Seen from this *different* perspective, pop music's practitioners and recipients have discovered that the involuntary, the appeal of a specific physicality, is more valuable than the skilful. They flaunt themselves, they are licentious, they flirt – but they produce no detachable, transportable objects; neither masterpieces nor trash. Rather, they produce countless fetishes and access points: links, relay stations, but hardly autonomous works – and it is not for nothing that the most work-like link in the pop music chain is called an 'album'. An album being a collection of memory-preserving photos.

Porn, reality TV, gastronomy, tourism, Tik-Tok and Instagram have long known about the economically expedient and extremely profitable resource of the involuntary, and have now, in the footsteps of pop music, developed vitality art into vitality marketing. Whether pop music has thereby become irrelevant or in need of change, whether it has ever been anything but a laboratory for exploiting the involuntary, as opposed to a genuine emancipatory machine, needs to be discussed.

Pop music makers must find techniques and methods of purposely manufacturing the involuntary, the alluring, the very fabric of desire – which is actually impossible. You cannot be purposely purposeless, you cannot craft a plan to wander aimlessly and get lost. The paradox that might help here is a device I call the pose: adopting a posture that can help make something involuntary happen. Mastering the act of passivity.

But some artists have better ideas of their own. Take Bo Diddley, who at the very start of his career, in the early days of rock 'n' roll, jiggles down the steps onto the stage to a seemingly endless West African-sounding guitar riff, and greets himself, his own artificial persona: 'Hey, Bo Diddley!' And his band answers: 'Hey, Bo Diddley!' This is the true self of pop music: a persona, totally fabricated and yet someone very specific, a fiction and yet an utterly unique character, ratified by a very specific physicality – that of Bo Diddley. However, he also needs the television set that enables him to propel sound and image, the singer, songwriter and guitarist Bo Diddley and the persona Bo Diddley, onto a public stage, whooped on by countless conspicuous teenagers in the audience, to whom the camera occasionally pans, simultaneously broadcasting them into cosy living rooms and bedrooms, where a teenager is sitting alone and not alone. This teenager will step out into the world, and will not only rediscover the source of the sound in public, but will also recognize for themself the squealing recognition performed by the teenagers on television – when he or she recognizes another or the same performer on another stage, and shouts: 'There he is!'

Listening to yourself remembering

Narcissism and self-reference are key elements of pop music's genesis and of the reference complex that constitutes it. The function of an electronic madeleine was first identified before pop music as I characterize it ever existed. In a very early essay,[1] Adorno explains how we hear technologically recorded music – and all pop music begins with a recording – no longer as music (that is, classical European music as he understands it: as a performance of a score in need of constant refreshment), but as a memory of a specific recording and thus as a memory of one's own specific hearing. He calls this effect the 'photo album': listening to recorded music on a record player or any other playback device is like leafing through a photo album. If I look at a photo of my husband in front of the Rialto Bridge or my wife on the Matterhorn, I see not the Matterhorn or the Rialto, but an indexical record of the physical presence of my spouse (and the photographer) on a specific day and in a specific place. Beethoven's piano sonata op. III is the Rialto; my listening to a recording by Glenn Gould of the same sonata, which I first listened to on Suarezstraße in Berlin through an open window at sunset one evening in early summer, corresponds to the Venice trip with my husband. But any disappointment with the loss of a very specific musical tradition through the (perceived) shift in its meaning – from reception as reconstruction of artistic intention, and of the supra-subjective plan that such works claim to follow – to pure narcissism via the technological medium of recording, fails to recognize that we still absolutely need the Matterhorn or the Rialto to make these people visible. We likewise still need music to create the connections that constitute pop music as a constellation, as a *dispositif*.

Billie and Lee: voice, percussion and effect

Let us cast our minds back for a moment to 2021. The teenage superstar Billie Eilish brings to market a new, widely acclaimed album (*Happier Than Ever*), masterful and artful in equal measure. And with the death of the reggae producer, writer, singer and visual artist Lee 'Scratch' Perry, Afro-Caribbean music loses one of its most important artists and innovators, a towering figure for his pioneering of dub. These two perhaps represent the poles of what I call pop music (as distinguished from rock, a subdomain of pop music, or soul, another subdomain, or popular music, a domain that intersects with pop music but is not identical to it; and as contrasted with pop culture, a misleading term that we must eventually return to; and as opposed to pop – a hazy prefix for all occasions).

What is striking about Billie Eilish is a particular artificial usage and staging of her voice. Its aesthetic precept lies not in the expansion or elaboration of musical possibilities: it is not about voice control, volumes or novel sounds; it is not about innovations that could plausibly be pinned down through notation. What is particularly striking about this is that it occurs in a segment of the pop music complex that appeals largely to a younger audience.

In every form of music, the voice represents the conjunction of what is naturally – and involuntarily – given as a precondition, with its use in artistic creation founded on learning, ability, knowledge and intention. This natural precondition, however, entails not only the physical laws of acoustics (as with a trumpet), but also a sentient human body. In pop music, the individual, contingent, mortal, specific body is more important than the learnable skills of mastering it or of mastering an instrument. The primary concern is the vestiges of the body captured through sound recording, albeit usually secondarily embedded in a – by no means arbitrary – musical performance. The relationship between musically describable elements and phonographically particular elements (i.e., what recording enables to be repeated and reproduced through the artist's body at the moment of recording, via the materiality of machines and instruments) can be balanced in innumerable ways: in terms of which is structurally dominant, which element governs the other and renders it intelligible, and also in terms of the percentage of music versus physical contingencies and/or specifics. In the case of Abba, for example, compositional and notational elements are almost entirely responsible for a song's success and reception, as with the hits and popular songs of the olden days; sound and recording are demarcated to the maximum:

the 'spectacle of the melody' (Terre Thaemlitz) dominates. In the case of J Dilla or Drake, by contrast, notable elements are negligible or cryptic in the extreme, eluding the instructional symbols of musical notation. Again, however, it would be a mistake to confuse pop music with pure sound art; just like music, it is sound art only in part.

Eilish performs an enjoyment of her own voice that is both historical and unprecedented. Such enjoyment was first exhibited in the 1950s by individuals – usually seen as hotheads or mavericks – who dared to use their individual, 'flawed' voices with confidence, despite having no formal vocal training. But these voices were often found at the fringes of society, ethnicized or marginalized by the mainstream. *Voice* was still bound up with *vote*: new voices signified a broadening of the democratic spectrum. In the 1960s and '70s, the age of counterculture and of men with long (feminine-coded) hair, using a 'weak' voice on the public platform became a sign of sensitivity; nasalization was cool (Bob Dylan, Ray Davies, Lou Reed), and even the loud, booming, often roaring voices that emerged in this period (Robert Plant, Roger Chapman,

Joe Cocker) were untrained. Soul singers were often technically superior, but responded to this development with an even greater explosion of diverse individual vocal qualities. However, the few women succeeding in pop music at the time still had conventionally beautiful voices on the whole, conforming to the gendered clichés of the girl or the diva (Judy Collins, Joan Baez) – the exceptions being those whose radicalism consistently surpassed that of their male colleagues (Linda Sharrock, Julie Driscoll/Tippetts, Yoko Ono, Patty Waters). At least since the 1990s, through idiosyncratic or even narcissistic vocal performances from artists like Björk and Joanna Newsom, there has emerged a female style of vocalization that tops the male self-indulgences of nasalization, grunting, whining and whimpering. This style exhibits a gratification in the sound of one's own voice as a mirror image of oneself, far surpassing the transgressions of '60s and '70s pop music in sonic and, more importantly, conceptual terms. Billie Eilish, though, unexpectedly brought this notion of 'singing in the mirror of one's own vocal cords' into the mainstream and into teen fashion – a boundary-shattering shift comparable with our newfound appreciation of defamiliarized special-effects voices and the application of autotune (most notably in R&B and hip-hop) in recent years.

To trace this brief (and of course abbreviated) historical outline, I have used barely any musical vocabulary, speaking instead of performative positions, behaviours and their relationship to bodies and particular social environments. This is no coincidence. Pop music is in large part what in China is known as *behaviour art*: the art of conducting oneself in a public setting. The term is by all accounts a 1990s retranslation of a Chinese expression, which itself originated as a translation of *performance art*. However, it captures the specific nature of pop music better than 'performance', which implies (predominantly) intentional acts and effects. Behaviour, when employed in art, works instead with presentation: offering glimpses, letting something happen rather than actively inducing it. Here, then, we have an apt name for this essential aesthetic strategy of seduction in pop music.

Besides voice, the beat – the part of the musical bedding that is not oriented in pitch, i.e. in conventional, predominantly European functional harmony – is vital to pop music's primary purposes, alongside other machine and sound effects. Of central importance are not only the rhythm of the beat and the influence of African and African Diasporic music (which is oriented in infinite rather than teleological musical time, thus laying the foundation for a fundamentally different mode of attention in pop music), but also – and this was one of the vital discoveries made by Jamaican dub producers – the *sound of the beat*, the beat as sound effect. The beat speaks (as it does in several African traditions).

These two effects, vocal effect and sound effect, are primarily indexical effects:[2] they speak of their causation – revealing through sound that they have specific human and/or mechanical-instrumental sources – more than they speak of artistic intention, as in the symbolic language of old European music-music, which tends to be more removed from the body. And yet they always remain connected to this music, only rarely straying from it towards noise or atonality or pure voice-beat combinations (as in some forms of hip-hop). However, there are also (as mentioned above) necessary non-sonic components without which pop music cannot function; unlike classical and classical popular music, it requires not only sound sources and listeners, but also images, language, ideas, costumes and stages.

Recording beyond nature and culture

However, the media-technological concept of recording is where it all begins. Recording brings into the accessible, readily available, stationary, sensual universe things that were not previously stationary: the uncontrolled motion of the external world, of life, of chance, of chaos. This chance moment, which was first frozen in the photographic image, was then set in motion again by new recording technology, remaining available and accessible on film reels and gramophone records, cassettes, VHS tapes, and so on. Aesthetics broached this watershed almost two hundred years ago: there now existed perceptible things that eluded its central distinction – art versus nature, or the beautiful versus the sublime. Recordings were traces, documents and symptoms of causation that were neither intentional (art) nor a product of fundamental laws (nature), and that could therefore be experienced as neither beautiful (art) nor sublime (nature). Neither the small subject (humans), nor the large subject

(God, the laws of nature, the 'big other' [Lacan]) lay behind them – only messy little causes, chains of events.[3] That is why the first question asked by any pop music recipient worth their salt is: Who is this person? What kind of person are they? Because such messy, possibly random or even accidental causation points towards the opposite of intention – i.e., a potential non-event – but is supposedly caused somehow by a human body (most probably by a voice), we want to know everything not only about the body, but also about the human. This jump from body to personality is logically flawed, but the logic of desire renders it quite compelling. It represents a central aporia of the pop music complex.

Although recordings were a source of great fascination from the outset, both as funfair attractions and as (scientific) documents, few questions were asked about their aesthetic novelty. At first nobody realized that they were experiencing a new type of aesthetic attraction. The possibilities of recording were considered, if ever they were linked to artistic practice or reception, purely in terms of the old arts. It was now possible to record a magnificent concert or to film a performance for future audiences, to reproduce a painting and circulate it widely in print – for all to see, not just the privileged few. It was generally believed that by recording art and music and reality, it would now be possible to prolong human activity, to preserve it better, to distribute it more easily, to make it accessible. Until the second half of the century, there was at best a sense that this offered a whole new type of enjoyment and appreciation – even aesthetic experience – but also a whole new form of exploitation of human physicality and presence.[4] The new recording media's potentially artistic character was given fullest consideration in the initially fastest-growing and most glaringly novel world of film, where a discourse had already sprung up around media specifics, though mostly limited (see Béla Balázs, Lotte Eisner and Rudolf Arnheim[5]) to defining and defending an inherent logic based on narrative and representation within filmic art (and its specific motions) as opposed to a theatre-oriented predilection for acting and dialogue – though still founded on the premise of a sovereign artist behind it all (usually considered to be the screenwriter). The exceptions to this were Eisenstein – whose theory of film attractions posited effect-oriented arguments, taking into consideration categories hitherto scorned in regular aesthetics, such as suddenness, surprise and overwhelmment – and most notably the circle around Georges Bataille,[6] who depicted the formless, the fluids seeping out of the body, the abjections challenging the anti-corporeal and iconocentric anthropomorphism contained in the Christian idea of the body as the image of God, and instead conceived a base materialism, finding artistic corroboration not least among surrealist photographers. The domain of the involuntary, of effects not caused by a sub-ject, of non-sovereign or semi-sovereign physical presence, which would later become so intrinsic to pop music, was beginning to emerge. Bataille's notion of 'formlessness' (*l'informe*) engenders the idea of a symptom[7] – an image that captures the indexical and involuntary essence of pop music appreciation, with its peculiar sounds, unusual voices, squeaks, noises and contortions.

Magic, misfits and mishaps

Features of this aesthetic emerged even before the gradual professionalization of the recording media began. The objective gaze of the camera and the objective ear of the microphone could record and thus evidence things, objectivizing their existence; things that not only resembled old funfair attractions – being more at home there than in official and recognized art forms – but that were likewise generally intended for a gullible, uneducated, infantile or marginalized audience. The effect was not far from deception: a magic trick simulating movement, the joy of which is nothing but pure movement; an 'abnormal' creature you might see at the funfair. Recordings showcased freaks of nature, bearded ladies, contortionists, people with peculiar qualities who did not conform to the normative ideal of the human body as an image of God: here were human beings, performers, making fools of themselves, doing ridiculous things, stumbling, grimacing. Magic, misfits and mishaps evolved strikingly from funfair attractions into more than a century of recording-media art to date – traceable from slapstick and what Tom Gunning called the 'cinema of attractions'[8] to Eisenstein's 'montage of attractions'[9] (an idea inspired by Meyerhold and circus culture), from Warhol's 'Screen Tests'[10] to present-day talent shows. The attraction of recording lies in vitality and motion, while motionless photographs capture the chaotic unpredictability of a single instant. Musical recordings, meanwhile, no longer record the work (as the score does); instead, they record a performance incorporating all manner of specific contingencies not marked in the score: tempo decisions, indispositions, ambience, and so on. All this opens the door to hitherto precluded effects, queer transgressions, forms of life and action that Western culture had previously tried, with success, to exclude from its art.

Mortality and death: ethnography, spiritism and voices

The earliest applications of sound recording beyond the reproduction and documentation of pre-existing art forms, and the briefly promising business model of marketing musicianless gramophone music for saloons, already implied a function that would enable a distinct aesthetic to form around them. In the early days, sound recording was utilized in scientific research involving marvels, magic and othering – in ethnography, in spiritism, and in the recording of historical voices (e.g., Caruso) – in other words, as a means of preserving life, of creating an indexical record (as in photography) of something singular – a once-mortal person – to preserve it beyond the grave. The oldest phonograph cylinder in the Berlin Phonogram Archive's invaluable collection contains recordings of indigenous dance music from British Columbia (1897), a theatrical performance from Bangkok (1900), a Kurdish singer's lament (1902), a Bondei xylophone piece from Tanganyika (1903), a mask-dance song from German New Guinea (1904), two professional string players from Uzbekistan (1905) and five Twi drum proverbs from Togo (1905), all taken in the first decade of their usage.[11] Beyond recording's application in colonial ethnography to construct, examine and objectivize a nonwhite-European other, the boom in spiritism around the turn of the twentieth century brought about repeated attempts to record the voices of the dead. This set the stage for later parapsychologists and clairvoyants, like the notorious Konstantin Raudive in the 1970s,[12] to promulgate the theory that otherwise inaudible voices from the beyond could be heard on tape recordings – though notably not on recordings specially planned for this purpose; they could only be heard by chance. The magical effects of recording only ever surfaced unintended. This too is a key aspect of pop music appreciation: what captivates us is – or so we imagine – produced unintentionally.

Ultimately, the wish to preserve the 'unforgettable Caruso' in the afterlife, thus preventing his voice from being forgotten, gave rise to what we now know as the star cult. At the heart of any recording is a specific person (or several people), with their own unique body – replete with its involuntary components – and with their own unique vitality and mortality. They are no longer defined and singled out by their ability, knowledge or virtuosity (i.e., what they can control), but by a special radiant attractiveness emanating from their own mortality; we admire them not as products of nature, nor for certain aspects of their being: their maturity, innocence or divinity. The star's personhood is, on the one hand, magical and bewitching, dangerous and endangered – close to death, even, because the durability of the recording foreshadows the physical death of its quarry – and, on the other, abstruse, aberrant and abject, an (erstwhile) object of othering and (colonial) ethnography.

A close relative of the star, and perhaps its predecessor, is a criminal on a wanted poster: his picture pops up all over the place, and meeting him in real life spells great danger and the need for caution. Andy Warhol was not the only one to see the connection between wanted posters and star cults. When a star made famous through photos and films and sound recordings appears in real life, audience members are similarly overcome by unexpected fervour, fainting by the dozen. The concepts of physically verifiable uniqueness (via fingerprinting, voice recognition, etc.) and certifiable individuality (consider the lip-sync scandals casting such individuality into doubt) are key elements of pop music.

Noise, makeup, ringing the bell: laboratory and studio, medium and form

The recording of sounds and images is comparable to the use of measuring instruments and laboratory equipment in science. Both are attempts to suspend the world, subduing an object so that it can be considered at leisure. Laboratory researchers strive to acquire new knowledge that can be applied scientifically and thus turned into information. In both the lab and the studio, a different temporality reigns than in the objects themselves: the opposite of real time.

In aesthetic terms, however, recording produces something more than just a record: it generates a certain type of otherness. The epistemology of laboratory and measurement (see Bruno Latour,[13] Karen Barad[14] and Quentin Meillassoux[15]) has noted this, taking it as the basis for new philosophical assertions – inquiring, for instance, as to whether an object of scientific scrutiny thus becomes a subject in its own right, and whether measurement (as opposed to conventional empirical knowledge) builds a bridge to the *thing in itself*, as in some forms of so-called speculative realism. One extreme of this otherness is noise, the old enemy of information in information theory; and pop music has birthed a whole subgenre devoted to noise, which began with aggressive sound effects and feedback taking on lives of their own (Stooges, Hendrix, etc.) and eventually, via the union of minimalism and rock (Velvet Underground, Lou Reed's *Metal Machine Music*), becoming an art form in their own right (especially in Japan through artists like Merzbow).

But, polar extremes aside, elements of noise and chance also exist within otherwise ordered iconic or symbolic worlds (images, notated sound) that in many respects conform to the standards of pre-recording media art. These same elements have become instrumental to the recording arts (pop music, film/video and photography), having remained purely incidental for a very long time – written off as unserious (i.e., too direct and therefore unartistic) effects (belonging at the funfair, not in art), or even as actual mistakes. They were the forerunners of the aesthetics of pop music: voice cracks, ambient noise, mimicry taking on a life of its own – signals that could trigger instant responses and even become deliberate selling points. These were direct forms of communication that were forbidden in art, breaching the barrier separating artistic communication from the speech act, from real life. No wonder Chuck Berry complimented his fictitious guitar hero 'Johnny B. Goode' on his ability to play the guitar 'just like ringing a bell'. A bell makes a pure sound, but one that performs a denotative message: Open the door!

For a long time, art could not accept or integrate such effects into its own self-image. At best, recipients sought to define an aesthetics of accident within the culture industry – of tolerated mistakes, of inability, of exuberance and other forms of (unplanned) directness, such as make-shift mixing. They came up with terms like 'trash culture' (with B-movies, budget productions and garage punk making especially heavy use of these special effects[16]) or even 'camp' – although camp not only craves and celebrates 'human' error in culture-industry products, worshipping it with almost fetishistic devotion, but celebrates even more the feverishly hasty plastering over of such effects as a new, thrilling effect of its own (consider the tons of makeup worn by Maria Montez which so moved Jack Smith,[17] or the comparable volume of sugary strings and winds that Phil Spector plasters on top of 'The Long and Winding Road'). This is not, however, to say that authenticity shines through only if we imagine the makeup isn't there. Rather, authenticity can only ever be revealed *ex negativo*: as more material is applied around the human head, around the face, the performer risks suffering an ever-greater fall: their humanness is thus emphasized far more than if they showed their bare face. The fact that they do not, and yet it still lies underneath – waiting for the right moment, playing the game of the pose – is the fractured-authenticity effect typical of pop music. Actively trying to be genuine, wanting to be genuine in the manner of Bruce Springsteen, is just authenticism. Ideology.

It may be instructive at this point to invoke the distinction between medium and form proposed by the German sociologist and systems theorist Niklas Luhmann.[18] A medium is anything that enables a form to emerge. Sound – the physical world of acoustics – is the medium that traditionally enables music's form to emerge. In pop music, this relationship is inverted: music is the medium, and what it gives form to is an indexical mode of relation to the real world, rendered fetishizable and attractive through music. Just as through a shell of makeup or a death mask there emerges the only face granted us that does not wither or age.

The laboratory equivalent here is a place that turns inanimate objects into agents (or, as Latour calls them, 'actants'): the recording studio. In very simplistic terms, if we can say that there is music, like European classical music, that rests on the interpretation of instructions (i.e., a score), and another sort of music, like jazz, that rests on playing together for a given length of time, then a third sort is music that occurs not in real time, but as a form of collective sculpture (by 'three-dimensionally' layering traces of things – tracks – one on top of another); the resulting recordings repeatedly and almost arbitrarily feature sound effects that leave a mark on the track as priceless as a voice from the dead: a colouration of sound or a fumbled chord, a bicycle bell or an electrically amplified yoghurt pot (in the case of the Beach Boys). The laboratory setting reinvents each sound – seldom with a planned effect in mind – as a targeted message from another ontology. As for the medium, what matters is that music is made, that instruments stand at the ready and are played, that microphones record and mixing desks process the tracks. The form emerges unpredictably against these continuities, routines and equilibria as the tape runs backwards.

Pop Music Belongs to the Second of Three Culture Industries

Culture industries and contradictions

At first, this concoction was left well alone by almost anyone claiming to be an artist (pop music artists tended to use the new possibilities selectively and tactically). The same could not be said of the new Taylorist Culture Industries, which integrated the recording media not into new artistic genres, but primarily into business models; the survival of traditional artistic formats and genres thus was coextensive with the application of new recording technologies. Cultural-industrial complexes tend to cast out spent or outmoded cultural commodities en masse – which has justifiably earned them a bad name among left-wing critics and right-wing culture pessimists alike. But engaging with the spent, the damaged, the simply structured, offers and offered the chance to shift the emphasis within it. The humble song could thus be transformed into a sort of reversible figure. The song's simplicity acquired great beauty through the fact that it now came to signify something beyond itself: it was an elegant (musical) structure that produced an (extra-musical) effect. However, this development – this unprecedented and unorthodox application of aesthetic refuse as the architectonic foundation of pop music's distinct character (and that of related industrial arts) – went unnoticed by culture industry theorists, who remained oblivious to developments and historical dimensions within the realm of the culture industry.

The culture industry was originally identified by its coiners, Theodor W. Adorno and Max Horkheimer, as a phase in the dialectic of enlightenment that succeeded other phases: it was thus a piece of history, in the lapidary sense of a succession of stages and periods. In it, however, they also saw the triumph of the capitalist law of value, which could now achieve total domination of the – possibly final – realm in which difference and self-will, resistance and dissidence still existed, at least in semantic terms: the realm of art. This is in a sense a post-historic endpoint. Then again – and this is a frequently raised objection – Adorno and Horkheimer's narrative overlooks the history of the means by which culture became a mass industrial phenomenon: through technological media, with its history of entanglement in capitalism, warfare and increasing productivity. For Adorno and Horkheimer, the culture industry is much more of an immersion in an omnipresent ideology than it is a historic and dynamic organization of mass cultural production and distribution – a business model based largely on proliferation and as such no longer available in the digital age (notwithstanding the differing business models of reproducing cultural commodities for individual sale – like books, magazines and records – and of access-based models financed by advertising [e.g., radio] or private subscription fees).

Today, the ubiquity of commodity and exchange is governed by a more developed, though no less capitalistic, business model, namely the trade in expectation and anticipation. Only from this phase of cybernetic capitalism can the

historicity of earlier phases of the culture industry be retrospectively examined. Surprisingly, it
is media scholars[1] – usually resolutely distanced
from historical thinking, favouring a positivist
advocation of largely contingent (technological)
progress – whose critique of the concept of the
culture industry allocates it a history. Wolfgang
Hagen has argued at length (in rebuttal to
Adorno) that radio is founded on quite distinct
technological standards, and consequently that
the suitability of radio devices and their usage
in the entertainment industry, advertising and
political propaganda does not simply follow a
single technological principle;[2] the Heideggerian
Friedrich Kittler[3] went even further in his
notorious global hatred of the Frankfurt School,
arguing that in the culture industry chapter of
Dialectic of Enlightenment, the term 'commodity'
should be replaced throughout by 'code'. 'Code'
would, in my opinion, initially disconnect the
commodity from its historicity, but would subsequently enable the relationship between code and
commodity to form a new dynamic of cultural-
industrial historicity (the numerous ways in
which code becomes commodity in film, sound
recording, photography and digital sampling is

half the story of culture industry history). So if we follow Kittler not to the end, but to halfway, we arrive not at a compromise between irreconcilable positions, but instead find material to elucidate cultural-industrial configurations as historical phases of the capitalist-cybernetic integration of art and culture.

The three culture industries

The first phase is the alliance of radio and cinema. Radio is an open, centralized platform of both propaganda and entertainment, often ceremonially staged, that conveys a constant stream of state rituals and acts of representation into the heart of the nuclear family. Its broadcasts carry into kitchens and bedrooms, where the commands and announcements of authority and time are received; the external order is then replicated and instituted in microcosm, though it remains flexible and adaptable to events behind closed doors. The emergent radio was joined by another institution, cinema, situated in exterior public space to which people make secular ceremonial pilgrimages in order to indulge in the most private pleasures and dreams – a sort of assisted dreaming that now occurred in public, in the dark, but in almost military synchronicity, in the funny parts and the tear-jerking moments alike.

These defining, formative, standardizing and regulating cultural institutions were built on the distinction between public and private: the combination of bedroom and theatre gave rise to the cinema; the conjunction of concert hall, barrack yard and family ritual produced the radio. The knowledge that such institutions can be built in this way helped develop the next phase of the culture industry, which now incorporated new knowledge that had played no part in the first phase, or rather had been unconsciously processed and absorbed. This knowledge appertained to the magical effect of dramatizing the indexical technological transmission of a real person – instead of neutralizing them for the sake of escapism and to be approved officially as family-friendly entertainment. In this new phase, radio and cinema lived on, but were now outshone by the new configurations of pop music and TV – compounds of media technology and social *dispositif*.

Television became the new radio, importing the public sphere into the family sphere – assuming the function of the fireplace, as McLuhan puts it – but it also invited the dream invocations of cinema into the home. Moreover, it established a new mode of relation to the people who appeared in media broadcasts. Recipients no longer languished in submission – the mode of reception for dramatic storytelling, as in French or Hollywood cinema of the 1930s and '40s – but instead felt a sense of ordinary everyday encounter, as familiar public personas were repeatedly conjured up before them, for instance in soap operas. Pop music exploited the same sense of unmediated access to people in recordings and media broadcasts, through the pairing of image and sound recording; it occupied no fixed location in public space (as cinema did), but initiated an ongoing relationship that could only ever be consummated by the recipients – fans passing through public space, who connected things they had heard in their bedrooms or recognized from television, magazines and records with new listening experiences in bars and at concerts – publicly showcasing themselves as consummate, card-carrying fans.

In Culture Industry II the indexical side – the sudden appearance of the directly broadcast or recorded person – takes centre stage. However, the person is neither ridiculous, hilarious or dangerous, as in the 'cinema of attractions', nor embedded in culture and narration, as in Culture Industry I. Instead, the magically unexpected moment now becomes the everyday motor of culture-industrial production; the person does not take the place either of the worshipped other-worldly diva (Greta Garbo) or of the 'ideal' guy and capable employee (Jimmy Stewart) in Culture Industry I, but is now, above all else, *real*: either real through material and physical flaws ('mistakes', 'cheapness', artlessness, the involuntary – all so cherished by camp reception) within the otherwise traditional staging of the soap; or real through their mundane ordinariness, their daily appearances, such as television presenters and daily soap actors whom some recipients almost know better than their partners; but above all else, real through the photographically and phonographically staged aggressive and sexual presence of the (usually male) pop star – vital, powerful, sexual and threatening.

The third culture industry is that of the Web 2.0, whose all-consuming integrating tendency is instantly apparent purely through the fact that wage labour and the reception of art increasingly take place on the same devices. For a while I believed that this new 'inside', a product of all-consuming integration, would give rise to a new 'outside' – as implied by the new possibilities of conquering an electronically taggable and monitorable outside world (Pokémon GO), the simultaneous boom in festivals like Burning Man, and more besides. Perhaps this 'outside' can no longer be conceptualized as an actual outdoor space. In Culture Industry III, pop music – a complex that emerged through

Culture Industry I	
Radio: SOUND, ordinary/ everyday, limited emphasis	*Cinema:* IMAGE, exceptionality, dramatic emphasis, idealization
Culture Industry II	
Television: IMAGE +, ordinary/ everyday, limited emphasis	*Pop music:* SOUND +, exceptionality, dramatic emphasis, physicality
Culture Industry III	
Internet: IMAGE +, SOUND+, ordinary/everyday, limited emphasis, dramatic emphasis	*Outdoors:* GPS, parkour, gatherings, events, exceptionality, physicality

In every culture industry, (1) elements of the social 'outside' breach the 'inside' of private/family life, and (2) an (autonomous or private or intimate) 'inside' breaches the social 'outside'.

its noticeable recipients moving visibly through public space – is finding itself stifled and at risk of imploding. It is impossible to tell whether it will survive this.

3

At the Heart of Pop Music Is No Object, but an Impulse to Connect

Configurations and constellations of the arts and media: linking and recognition

Cinema is not a standalone medium; it is the practice of not just one art form, but several. Similarly, pop music is technically speaking not a single medium, but a nexus of several media. Unlike cinema, however, the configuration of its technical apparatuses and architectures is inconsistent. Instead, its apparatus is a social one: the shifting social world. Pop music is entirely constituted by articles that are either open-ended or perceived as incomplete – each of which makes reference to others, offering to integrate them into the reception experience via the act of recognition: *ah, this beat is from that film where that person has the hairstyle I was looking at when I heard this voice.* Pop music is a constant, dynamic virtual amalgamation of diverse media and sign systems from the real world (more on this in a moment).

This sounds fragile, delicate – volatile, even. But let us note that our object of comparison, cinema, is a *remarkably* stable concept, given the long and fluid list of its various (media) components throughout history. Despite the existence of many different concepts, conventions and media principles – from 'bioscope' to 'film theatre' – the prevailing opinion remains that the 'history of cinema' spans all the way from the funfair attractions of early moving pictures right up to private home cinema streaming today; everything in between falls comfortably under the umbrella term of 'cinema'. In terms of individual disciplines, cinema incorporates a vast array of artistic endeavours (dance, singing, acrobatics, literature and fiction, screenwriting, pantomime, painting, set design, and so on), media (photography, sound recording, celluloid strips, etc.) and conventions regarding its public presentation, distribution and business model (forward-facing seats, a dark room, a projector, access via ticketed entry and later via individually sold copies on VHS and DVD). However, the precise combination of rented celluloid copy, exposed moving image, dark room, projection, and a dramatic plot of a defined standard length has formed a media-technological-artistic-economic constant, creating a socially established centre that merges all these components and can be sought out in certain locations.

Pop music is a similar combination. That is to say, it is constituted by a similar quantity of different components at different levels. Unlike cinema, however, it has no centre, not even a shifting centre – neither a central object nor a central creator. In dialectic terms, this is the true heart of pop music – or at least it remained so for a long time. Pop music has its roots in a form of *linking*, which (unlike internet links) leads not to an equivalent (i.e., to further digital data), but instead to a diverse range of cognitive associations – from sound to image, from solitude to society, from purchasable playback device to immaterial habitus – by means of musically prompted *recognition*. The cognitive reflex of recognition is, as it were, the hardware behind these links.

Recognition exploits a media discovery that dates back to early talkies, but that only became visible in the 1950s with the omnipresence of radio, recording devices, film, photography and television. It was the discovery of our consistent ability to recognize acoustic phenomena via visual cues, and vice versa. This established the notion of recognition across media formats as an everyday phenomenon with an increasingly important role to play in negotiating everyday life. However, the linking process does not stop at recognition; it merely uses it as a conduit. Nor is a link just a sign: it not only refers to something, but forges a real-world relationship with the object of reference. As an 8-year-old I rummaged for specific pieces of clothing to replicate the Beatles' outfits, assembling my idea of a convincing Beatle suit. And needless to say, I cut my long hair when Lou Reed's *Transformer* came out.

A consequence of this linking process is that there is no dominant artistic discipline within pop music either. No pre-eminent authorial position (e.g., producer, director, songwriter) holds absolute sway (though power grabs have been made from each of these positions). However, the most pervasive tendency throughout the history of pop music is the attempt – analogous to the construction of its main attraction, the indexical transmission of a human body – to relate the constituent parts of pop music (or at least its production) to the person (or people) performing or representing it. The void at the heart of the pop music complex is offset by the fantasy of the totally authentic pop star. Someone who starts out just as a singer soon becomes a songwriter, ideally a producer too, and later a director of their own videos or rock operas. This gives rise to the paradox that pop music artists want ever more command and control (of composition, production, set design, video shoots, etc.), and yet they increasingly (and necessarily) relinquish what they cannot control.

In a TV documentary, two female fans of a male rapper were asked what they loved so much about him. Fan A said that he was completely himself: he didn't try to repress or control his personality, but laid it bare for all to see. Fan B stated that every aspect of him was curated and that he maintained complete control of his appearance and his impact. In the search for the heart of pop music, this forms a perfect vanishing point: the moment when total control and total lack of control converge.

Recipients built the pyramids

The principles of pop music production mean nothing without recipients. To avoid misunderstandings, let us first note two points about pop music reception. First, broadly speaking, I am indebted to Kant's aesthetics of reception, which consider art not in terms of normatively describable objects, but in terms of subjective experiences. However, I do not see the recipient's role as consistent across *all* art, pop music included; instead, I shall propose a fundamental difference: most other art forms present recipients with a given object, whereas pop music can only be brought into existence through the reception process itself. Second, notions of 'activated' and 'active' fans, so cherished by cultural studies theorists like John Fiske, are of no concern here. In pop music, the activated fan is the rule, not the exception. Fans do not even need to be especially fanatic; they can play the role of recipient – providing the final link in the pop music complex – just by indifferently driving to work with the radio on, listening with half an ear to a recent hit. An image will form before their eyes, a pattern of behaviour will gradually take shape – and only then is the (perhaps totally insignificant) song complete.

That said, pop music recipients are people who can delineate its aesthetic categories very precisely, as we saw in the previous chapter. These categories are especially unusual because they form criteria by which to judge not virtuosi, not works, not products of nature or creation, but human beings (Bo Diddley or Billie Eilish). Recipients follow links that forge connections with images, performances, (usually popular) music recordings, indexical sound effects, texts and stories involving real people. This vast cultural programme of artistically mediated de- and/ or re-programming, beginning around 1960 in the shadows and side rooms of official institutions, went undetected at first. The only observations made were either sociological ('youths', 'teens', 'generations', 'unemployed', 'middle-class', 'deviant') or musical ('rock 'n' roll', 'primitive', 'rhythmic', 'syncopated', '32 bars'). Essential connections – between, for example, watching a television broadcast of a filmed stage show; listening to a multitracked studio recording on a stereo system in your parents' living room, or a smaller device in your bedroom; listening to a radio programme in an older friend's car as you drive into town; attending a live concert by a band or artist whose studio recordings you have listened to on repeat on your Walkman; wearing certain clothing associated with an icon on an album cover; cultivating a certain posture to express stoned apathy, indifference and a dislike of sports; putting on kohl makeup as a cis boy or bright blue eyeshadow as a 13-year-old girl; smelling the same things at meeting spots in town, where the song you heard yesterday on the radio is being played; i.e., the non-arbitrary relationship between public listening, communal listening and listening in the privacy of your own room – all these connections are made not by a medium, not by analogy, not even by an ideology, idea or inclination, but by recipients themselves: the fans, the lesser-integrated and therefore ideologically relatively independent customers of pop music. This makes for an apparently ephemeral and changeable social web of endlessly varied pop music experiences. At the same time, however, there emerge distinct physiognomies that come to characterize certain eras, styles and attitudes – that can be spoken of as historical phenomena in the same way as particular schools of Renaissance art.

The attempt to understand pop music, to reconstruct its constituent parts, usually forms part of a process of world-making undertaken by people who are not yet or not at all integrated into social institutions (work, employment, occupations, etc.): young people, recent immigrants, discriminated minorities. Their mode of relation to the world is to be alone in society – not entirely alone, not a complete stranger, but alone in relation to the well-oiled machine of society operating around them; they are simultaneously without and within. By recognizing sonic and other sensory impressions (usually powerful ones), they see and make connections, serving to counter their loneliness – creating not only credible connections that strengthen their sense of orientation, but also outlets for their desires – enabling them to 'come out', in the queer sense, from the particular isolation of youth and discrimination. The route from inside to outside – the connection between the private bedroom experience of recorded voices and sounds, directed at me and me alone, to and with the public experience of encountering the same voices and sounds – is the prototype of this 'alone in society' scenario, and means two things. First, the people who go to bars and listen to the same music as I do in my bedroom are my people; but my solitary experience still precedes the communal one, and underpins it; I am with them and yet alone. Second, the people who listen to the same music in public as I do alone, the same voices, were also alone at first, like me; so they are my people; we are alone together, with society around us.

But music also imposes this sense of loneliness when an untouchable human body speaks to me alone at night, simultaneously comforting me and yet emphasizing my aloneness as the basis of this communication. The activities, projections and desires of the recipient are thus the primary concern. Recipients are the users, but also to a vast extent the makers of pop music. Its grand liberating powers, its extremely attractive promise (and more often than not its big lie) that it can provide real use values within consumer capitalism, can only be ratified and fulfilled by its users. (This requires them to take the queer step of detaching themselves from the lives that society has preordained for them along class and discrimination lines.)

Music as default storage

It would be impossible to describe pop music in language designed solely for understanding music and its traditions. It would be equally impossible, however, to describe pop music without music. At a functional level, music is the ideal storage medium for the plethora of different things (images, ideas, memories, noises, physical feelings) that flow between the various transmitting and receiving stations of the pop music network. This is precisely because people can store and reproduce music without the help of technology. Music generates cognitive linking codes. People know tunes by heart. Musical shapes are not only ideal mnemonics – in the sense that we can easily internalise melodies and similar sequential patterns – but they are also ideal in terms of connectivity: music latches on to other perceptions and extra-musical cognitive processes like a piece of blotting paper. The arrival of sound recording, however, reinvented this process in a way that became intrinsic to pop music. Recorded music shares its patterns of attraction with other media that record life, contingency, chance, physicality, the involuntary and the unintentional. It generates a new relationship between the listener and the listened-to in which the listeners themselves, their own listening, play a new role. It is an industrial madeleine in both the productive and the conditioning sense.

We know that music works especially well as a medium for sound, noise and stirring real-world causes when it is played quite conventionally, and when the music itself is not muscled into the limelight. This is why it is largely conventional and traditional (or traditionally presented) musical forms, widely popular forms of diverse origin – predominantly African American, but also Irish, Hillbilly and various hybrids – in which recorded music's central attraction of the transmitted body is embedded. However, it is not only through traditional form and structural simplicity that music becomes better suited to embedding the effects of body and presence, by retreating into the background and remaining unmarked; in pop music especially, there are more factors in play. The rustic precursors of rhythm and blues were first recorded partly from an ethnographic perspective – an ethnographic perspective that had always had a special relationship to real-world causes in recordings. Othering in ethnomusicology – however noble and philanthropic the motives of some of its representatives like Alan Lomax may have been – coded experiences of the effects of body and presence differently, racializing or othering them in various ways (as backward, primitive, genuine, authentic, and so on). Nevertheless, many musical styles developed in African Diasporic cultures lend themselves extremely well to pop music, not because (as standard para-racist white rock ideology would have it) they are so raw and honest and authentic – but because they are structured non-teleologically. They are not founded on a model of tension and (re)solution from a single perspective; instead, their structure is fundamentally open-ended and incomplete. In ordinary pop music, the lines have frequently become blurred and confused between the actual artistic significance of African American and African Diasporic music in relation to all pop music, and the ideological veneration of a racialized, ethnographically constructed notion of Black authenticity.

Many musical commentators, scholars and critics still try to infer the effects of pop music entirely from the musical content of the music, only to be flummoxed by the fact that what sounded new in the 1950s, and had novel effects on its audiences, was not musically new at all – at least as far as notational aspects of the music were concerned. Ethnographic othering (ingrained in the phenomenon of the real world, insofar as it appears in music) has more often than not been inverted by pop music into self-othering, self-ethnicization and tribalization. Obviously, there are significant differences between white and nonwhite perspectives on ethnicization and self-ethnicization: people who have never been ethnicized or racialized will naturally have more fun passing off their festivals as a 'Gathering of the Tribes'.

As a medium, music possesses a certain non-innocence, in the sense that as soon as it gives form (in the sense of the medium/form distinction) to real-world effects, it finds itself confronted once again with its own ethnicized history. Pop music counters this by attempting to ascribe music and real-world causes to one source, one point of origin: the pop star, the performer – thus running straight back into the other big (though less pressing) problem, that of ideological authenticism. A music that is used as a medium, rather than a form, need not be founded on conventional and/or traditional formats. Pop music also often relies on an understanding of music no longer as the expression of a single subject, but as an expression of the world, of the great beyond, of the planet, of the ecosystem. This idea has shaped the whole of the last century – from Debussy's *La Mer* to Varèse and Cage, from ambience to minimalism. In pop music, alongside the fundamental orientation around non-European, non-teleological music, these traditions have become instrumental – especially since the mid-1970s and early '80s, when pop musicians more or less figured out for themselves what they actually do. Embedding, connectivity and linking are not music's only function within pop music; as we shall see later, it always involves differentiation and secession too.

Recognition

As we have seen by now, the topic of pop music can only be discussed with due consideration for the music itself, but the discussion does not revolve around musical effects: rather, the music is a vehicle or a bedding; again, in Luhmann's terms, it is a medium, not form. Its core functional principle – enacted when the music is listened to – is enabling a recording to be recognized, read and translated into other languages, categories and sign systems. We now know that this works across media formats, and that pop music takes advantage of it: in the 1950s, billions of people gaped at suddenly enlarged four-colour record sleeves replete with photos, as they listened to music by singers they knew from television, with sound effects they knew from the radio (if not from places in town). But in a deeper sense, why is it so stimulating to realize that we have recognized someone or something? Well, the stimulus is strongest when we have no *tertium comparationis* – no concept, no name, at best perhaps a proper name – to describe what connects the then and now, the here that reminds us of there. This immobilizes the connection and renders it operational. The unlabelled and unnamed then makes the supra-linguistic content of consciousness available through a sound memory stored in a specific location. It can do this not only with content that we remember; it also makes future content conceivable, connecting what is linguistically indeterminate but specifically available through sound (or music?) with intuitions and wishes directed towards the future or projecting onto it – projecting its promises.

Dogs have no vocabulary, and yet they have a precise sense of orientation through smell and memory, which perhaps forms the template for their memory techniques. Early pop music echoes the very popular but highly peculiar idea that a dog is best at confirming the authenticity of a sound recording (see His Master's Voice). Gertrude Stein's famous witticism 'I am I because my little dog knows me' rests on the conclusiveness of nonconceptual recognition. The little dog also gives existential meaning to what is heard: the master is everything to the dog; the dog's life depends on them. Hearing is the primary sense, the one that warns us of danger, because unlike eyesight it is essentially omnidirectional. Music has shut down the warning dimension of sound through its mathematical and symbolic generation of meaning, but sound recording gives this dimension renewed importance: *what was that noise?* Music listeners find themselves constantly in recognition mode anyway – because you always listen to music several times. That is the point of it. But only since the arrival of recorded music can we recognize specific moments, specific living bodies, specific instruments, rather than just melodies, timbres and genres. What connects us to them has no name, no scale: we are the dogs to these new masters. Such was the state of things in the first half of the twentieth century, roughly speaking. It is no wonder that pop music, *musique concrète* and John Cage's 'small sounds' emerged in the middle of that century: they all work with the excess of specificity and physicality that recording makes possible. But while Cage and Pierre Schaeffer ramp up references to the outside world, only to separate them again from the meaning of the world – in their work, we supposedly do not *recognize* the noise, but hear it as a certain uncertainty, rich but diffuse in meaning – pop music develops a whole system of references that is constantly expanding, opening up to more and more contingencies. Looking back today on its history, we might accuse pop music of having spun its users into an unrealistic or commodity-like cocoon – or else of having an empowering effect by turning the connection, the link, into form.

Interconnection, mass identification and engagement

In the first half of the century, recognizable voices were identified only with the recognizable bodies they belonged to. Although the act of listening to music had transformed in the narcissistic sense described by Adorno, sound traces still pointed predominantly towards a body marked out for nothing other than its music-making abilities (as mentioned, in early recordings this was qualified by ethnographic and voyeuristic aspects, and by melancholic mourning for the future death of the recorded person). However, after the end of the Second World War, there was an explosion in the quantity of references to these bodies across diverse media formats, and also in recipients' ability to recognize voices and noises no longer just as individuals, but (because there were so many of them) as examples of something larger – something defined not by artistic and stylistic choices, but by its practical, everyday, existential significance: voices were now linked to habitus, protest, noncompliance, seduction, coolness and so on. Interconnected media outlets such as magazine images, television images and images on record sleeves that were no longer generic, but specially designed, supplied a constant stream of new physical depictions of pop musicians. Moving images in particular, which (not least through the new medium of television) provided increasingly vivid information about living musical sound sources – through the presentation and representation of musicians' bodies – conditioned audiences in a new process of recognition across media and genres. A voice was no longer recognized just as a voice, but as the voice to accompany this hip wiggle, the voice to this haircut, the voice to this outfit. Likewise, a fashion statement brought to mind the voice of the outfit, the voice of a style, a unique physicality, all of which recipients grasped without needing to be diverted by verbal or even conceptual cognitive operations.

We are not yet speaking of *production* formats – which are a congenital part of pop music and did not exist before its emergence – but for now let us at least consider this: from a production perspective, a plausible umbrella term for the culture of connection and linking on the recipients' part would be the 'aesthetics of *Verabredung*'. The German word *Verabredung* means something different and something more than its closest English equivalents, 'date' on the one hand and 'appointment' on the other. It suggests both a private, possibly erotically charged arrangement to meet, and a cooler, more business-like, even juridical, agreement to undertake joint or reciprocal action. The amalgamation of 'date' and 'appointment' lies at the heart of band culture aesthetics: a band performs a unified action at an agreed time – from doo-wop to the British Invasion and beat music, to the conceptual postpunk of Pere Ubu and The Jesus and Mary Chain; band members are young people empowering themselves by joining forces (and occasionally harmonizing) – usually men without training or special abilities, but with a flair for new forms of connection. *Verabredung* is the primary social behaviour at the onset of self-organization and empowerment (as opposed to the synchronic organization of employment, sports and the military); its encroachment into the aesthetic realm marked the beginning of pop music. Musical cultures of *Verabredung* were always linked to propensities for harmonized clothing, specific poses and fine-tuned facial expressions on record covers. This continued to develop in the 1960s far beyond the pop music world – as, for example, in the famous group photo of the Seth Siegelaub Gallery conceptual artists Robert Barry, Douglas Huebler, Joseph Kosuth and Lawrence Weiner.

4

An Assembly of Effects and Small Noises

Social visibility

Listeners of pop music in the 1950s thus aurally connected voice characteristics and individualities with other (visually perceived) physical traits, but also with general statements – exemplified by the much-discussed 'youth styles' that became an object of scrutiny in cultural studies.[1] But most research understandably confined itself to specific historical pop music cultures (often in Great Britain), without taking into account the culturally further-reaching media-systemic dimension of pop music. This dimension reaches beyond binary connections across media and genres (stylistically mediated attitudes and behaviours on the one hand, musically mediated physicality and embodiment on the other – subject to the conditions of race, class and gender). Further connections emerge through the diversification, fluidization and pluralization of social spaces in music – in terms of both rituals and media technology. Listening devices became smaller and transportable (portable record players and transistor radios were followed by boom boxes, the Walkman, iPod and other MP3 players), and jukeboxes popped up everywhere, creating new public forms of listening to recorded music. The short-lived phase of so-called 'soundies' (visual jukeboxes that played short, simple little films of musicians) set the stage for the ever-stronger presence of pop musicians on television. In the USA, the 1950s brought regular and frequent opportunities to see the pop stars of the day as moving bodies, broadcast in quick succession, with each act filmed differently (*American Bandstand*). West European television networks, mostly publicly owned, followed just under a decade later with regular programmes of their own (*The Old Grey Whistle Test*, *Beat Club*). In addition, many pop stars then began to appear in feature films, especially in the late '50s when Elvis Presley's film career took off. They appeared sometimes as themselves, sometimes as fictional characters from another world entirely, and sometimes as fictional pop musicians. This newfound visibility – offering up detailed, high-resolution objects of projection, revealing in high-definition what could previously be signified only via sound signals from the radio and jukebox – created an abundance of tangible objects that could only be absorbed and productively transformed by the socially mediated space in which they were shown. Pop music was everywhere, and its loci were linked by catwalk-like routes trodden by conspicuous young people (or at least, young people paranoidly believing themselves to be conspicuous), leading in turn to increased and increasingly charged recipient activity: fan culture. Meanwhile, the visual culture of pop music and its primary medium of the album cover could by the mid-1960s be split into three main genres: portraits of people or groups of people whom the recipients desired ('That's who I want'); portraits of people or groups of people who served as role models ('That's who I want to be', 'That's who I want to transform myself into'); and – in an initially mostly psychedelically coded additional step – images of spaces that people wanted to enter or be immersed in ('That's where I want to be'). These visual genres were the culmination of a new mode of reception arbitrated by an urban, social spatiality shaped by pop music ('Dancing in the Streets'). Over the course of the 1960s, visual genres developed into cinematic genres of their own, evolving in various ways out of experimental film – from *Chumlum* (Ron Rice, with music by Velvet Underground founding member Angus MacLise) and *Flaming Creatures* (Jack Smith) to so-called Expanded Cinema and psychedelic feature films, from *More* to *2001*. In the '70s, the immersive world was joined by the worlds of nostalgia and fantasy, laying the foundations for later cultures of interconnection in the digital age.

This trio of album cover types was not totally stable, however. The images – borrowed from the old culture industries – of a (usually female) star to be worshipped and desired, and a (usually male) star to be identified with, and of landscapes to be conquered and populated somehow (in the colonial, adventurous sense) became jumbled up in various ways in pop music. Authentic, indexically transmitted bodies were layered with

makeup borrowed from the old culture industry. This dialectic gave rise to queer transgressions
as early as Elvis: the man with whom recipients
were supposed to identify now concealed his
physical imperfections, much like the woman
whom recipients were supposed to desire under
the old regime. Boundaries were blurred between
the male gaze and a newly emerging female gaze
(which we will discuss later). The space inviting
recipients to immerse themselves – as seen on
prog-rock covers and in the Stargate scene in *2001*
– was no longer a colonial space to be conquered
through adventure, but a passivating one, where
the conqueror would be sucked in, enclosed
by new (and presumably moist) surroundings,
exposed, and swallowed up.

Teenage bedrooms: vestibules of society

With its diverse array of outlets, pop music no
longer just represented the relationship of voice
characteristics and sound effects with behaviours,
opinions, styles and stances; it also linked them
to social listening formats, social structures and,
most importantly, the routes between them.
From the white middle-class perspective (which

is the most documented, though not the most significant, except insofar as it provided major economic impetus in the 1950s when pop music first emerged), cultures of interconnection can be boiled down to a crucial paradigmatic psychological act, performed en masse at the time by so-called teenagers. This act was the recognition of a specific and physically present voice, and of certain sound effects, that the teenager had first encountered in a very intimate and private space (their childhood bedroom) and now recognized in public, where they met other people. In these very formative phases of subjectivation and adolescent development, pop music created very specific connections between episodes of individuation and socialization; other connections built on less polarized connectors essentially followed this model.

Music, especially popular music, has in a sense always played a part in the development of young people, albeit one rooted in another mediality and functionality. The song I danced to when I met a sweet boy would have been played by local musicians at the café, carnival or fair. I could commit only the melody to memory, and when I re-encountered that melody in another place, I recalled it in a much weaker sense than I would have done if I had heard a recording – let alone if this recording were impregnated with other meanings (images of people, behaviours, ideas). The dawn of pop music broke only gradually, as specific recordings took hold; but its musical material – popular music – had long since had a role to play in the life organization of unintegrated people.[2]

As these segments of the population waited in the vestibules of society, imagining and projecting their future lives, the participatory activation of pop music alerted them to their status and to newfound possibilities of connection with real life. They grasped that indexically recorded sounds and images must somehow unfold their full explosive power in social spaces as soon as they were able to meet other people. In a manifesto penned jointly in 1964, the musician, mathematician, artist and coiner of 'concept art' Henry Flynt and the Fluxus 'chairman' George Maciunas claimed that the pop music heard on the streets, and the listeners embodying and emanating it, especially African American youths, were a kind of vanguard of the American working class – a fact that sluggish party communists had not yet twigged.[3] A prevalent feature of this revolution was young people carrying around radios, and later cassette machines; Jacques Attali interpreted countercultural listening habits as a historical extension of other noise riots, such as the Charivari tradition.[4] The other side of this aloneness in society was implemented technologically by the Walkman and its many digital successors: now it is no longer *we* who are alone in society, but *me*. I no longer communicate my interconnectedness and my routes through society, but my depressive introversion – which only works in pop music if I show it on the outside. The Walkman came into the world to play Joy Division.

Singularity and authenticity

A comparable process is observable in other musical genres. Leaving the diva cult aside for a moment, there are of course fans of singers, conductors and instrumentalists in classical music, traditional popular music, the so-called Great American Songbook and folk music who are equally mesmerized by vestiges of their idols in particular recordings.[5] These recipients are

undeniably similar to their pop music coun-
terparts. However, producers of classical music
recordings endeavour to utilize such moments as
means to musical ends. The object of the fans'
desire is contained within the aesthetic object-
ives of the music and its performance. The arrival
of sound recording in the technological era
reinforced this, but only circumstantially. The
singer's timbre, Sonny Rollins's saxophone tone,
the pianist's touch: in semiotic terms, these too
are indexes, specific intimations of causation. In
pop music, however, these are no longer defined
by musical considerations – at most, they are
framed, abetted and underpinned by them. As
for production aesthetics, the challenge is: how
can I draw maximum attention to the appearance of an index, of a real-world cause (preferably
an involuntary, perhaps not entirely controlled
human behaviour, or an unforeseen social situation)? Pop music points entirely towards the
phonographically specific, to contingent singularities that the recording process captures and
renders audible. As a result, the singularities
(the performing individual, the social situation,
the technological-social studio environment,
etc.) must interact with a music suitable for this

purpose. Because this music cannot anticipate the exact details of the event it will accompany, evoke, underpin or support, it must not be too specific. At the same time, it must have character, and the musical bedding must contain interpretative aids for the contingent and potentially almost meaningless event – symbolic and visceral aids to the real world. This is why resolutely monotonous, enthusiastic but crudely simple patterns have proved to be an unbeatable recipe for pop music: think of 'Rumble', 'Louie Louie', 'Sister Ray', James Brown, The Fall, Schoolly D, Suicide – right up to techno, where irreducible, singular events are often to be found no longer on the recording, but only in the reality of the rave. The crudeness of the musical bedding thus provides a great, powerful platform for 'small sounds' and sound events; it manages, by not pretending to be anything else, to exclude all the boring people out there who want music-music – thus fulfilling the tribalist obligations of every youth- or counterculture.

By contrast, music that addresses the media-technological situation created by recording, taking into account the new (potentially auratic) role of contingent singularities (a modernistic approach typical of John Cage's work) – or that, in line with the principle of aleatorics, seeks to organize and thematize chance – is pursuing a different end. This kind of music seeks to transform chance, everyday contingencies and vitality into new *musical* material, rather than letting music convey it as what it is. It seeks intentionally to produce the real (in Lacan's sense of the word) for a purpose – to do it justice. From the institutionally and culturally secure and unambiguous position of the composer, phonographic singularities play a part within or as the composition itself. In pop music, the phonographically specific means not a phonographic accident that is subsequently recorded and processed, but a technologically reproducible unreproducible effect that relates to a very specific, previously introduced or generally imaginable person, place, group or situation. It is deliciously random and unpredictably vital only *in relation to* its origins. The phonographically specific can only emerge in connection with constants and conventions; pop music seeks to organize this.

It does so largely without self-reflection, generally remaining unaware of what it is doing. As soon as it senses its own function, it tends to become Cage, as almost happened with John Lennon's 'Revolution 9' – and as is observable in the noise genre that has been growing for more than twenty years, and especially in Japan.[6] Pop music can be similarly disrupted by commercial interests that seek to market the allure contained within traces of a one-off real-life event, and by the artistic convention that misguidedly seeks to ascribe this allure to learnable skills or brilliant individual accomplishments. But its greatest problem lies in the fact that alongside the specificity of phonographic recording, pop music must also encourage a specific relationship to the world – if it wants to do more than just presenting documents for appraisal. To become anything like art, it must help to shape a world whose traces constitute its own substance – and it must do so from its blind spot, from a position of ignorance, from the mistaken belief that it is only music. In reality, it utilizes live performances responding to recordings in a particular way, images implying a visual environment in which specific one-off sounds were made, and rituals and rhythms whose dominance enables us to imagine a life real enough to leave such inimitable traces.

At the very moment when pop music seeks to determine and take responsibility for life – the contingencies and indeterminacies of which constitute pop music's own essence – it runs the risk of authenticism, i.e. the danger of treating suggestive signs, traces of reality, as something absolute, reifying them and thus falling prey to the misconception that the life attested by phonographic traces must be a very specific and special one and can be understood as intentionally responsible for its attractiveness. Such authenticism is the opposite extreme from the Cage scenario. Pop music must prevent itself crumbling into this authenticism just as it must prevent its transformation into music-music (if it wants to remain itself and fulfil the format that marks it out from others). Where authenticism begins, the culture industry, politics, culture struggles, rebellion, self-fulfilment, subjectivization and other complexes also rear their heads.

The case against phoniness: youth culture and counterculture

One of pop music's central contradictions is that authentic traces of a performer's body can be misconstrued as evidence of a recording's moral or aesthetic sincerity. Its aesthetic task emerges from this contradiction: pop music has to develop a reflexive approach in relation to the fetishization of the apparent congruence of media authenticity and content authenticity; it is thus both a contradiction and an opportunity. In the early days, pop music was still wrestling with a cultural environment characterized by double standards and petit-bourgeois roleplay, as famously explained by Erving Goffman, among others.[7] The familiar historical problems of double standards, the authoritarian personality and *phoniness*, as it came to be known, could be countered efficiently by weaponizing physical integrity: this was intrinsic to the concept of rock 'n' roll and its working-class cultural dimension, and suited the media format of pop music. This same authenticism was later (not very much later) deployed as a homophobic, transphobic, antifeminist regressive norm – though that was not explicitly on the agenda of what started life as a cis-male heterosexual culture of liberation.

Most early attempts to explain the beginnings of pop music and its culture revolved around two factors: the civil rights movement in the

USA, and the increased buying power of young people – i.e., the specialization of an expanding hedonistic leisure market for more precisely defined and targeted consumers. But the ban on tobacco and alcohol sales to young people, and parents' apparent bigotry with regards to the civil rights movement, were the only examples of the older generation's *phoniness* that could be explicitly addressed. They could easily be met with direct and substantial challenges such as those from (among others) Eddie Cochran[8] regarding the former, and Bob Dylan[9] regarding the latter. The development of pop music, and of the genres that evolved alongside it, was part of a wider claim to truth forming in the younger generation; pop music emerged in conjunction with emerging teenage and countercultural social forms that upheld, promoted, processed and lived this claim to truth. This claim per se was always stronger than the content of any specific truth that it articulated. Belief in the indexical truth of voice transmission, and in the honest immediacy of the singing body, fomented attitudes so uncompromising that no amount of argument or manipulation could change them. Or so young people felt. But this was more than just a pastime and a craze; this was the stuff of which counter-cultures as we know them are made.

We cannot simply slap the rather bombastic label of 'counterculture' onto pop music's entire social history – at least not without a few words of explanation. 'Counterculture' implies two substantial claims: first, that there is a place outside or at the edge of normal (social) goings-on that is not only divergent from the rest, but actively antagonistic towards it; second, that this antagonistic force has something to do with culture, that its antagonism actually feeds off its culture. Both claims require qualification and explanation, which I will come to later – though I will ultimately insist on retaining the term.

Re-emergence of the high–low divide

Armed with this claim to truth, pop music re-enters the distinction between popular and elite culture, between high and low, into popular culture itself. In two ways. First, it essentially declares that popular culture in its historical or existing form has failed to do its job as the culture of the people – the culture of directness, of ordinariness and so on (it is too conformist, it has 'sold out' and become 'industrialized', reactionary or bourgeois). Pop music counters with a more direct, sexual, physical and ordinary popular culture that finds its cutting edge in the indexical transmission of bodily signals. Second, it challenges popular culture (a dull, consensus-based mass culture) using smaller countercultural entities based on more complex cultural practices (a model envisaged by some optimists on the left), thus offering a more authentic culture of the people – a countercultural avant-garde to supplant a levelled-out mass culture governed by the culture industry.

In the same timeframe (at least since the 1950s) a similar process has been observed within high culture (literature, cinema, theatre, visual art), with exponents challenging the claims of existing culture or holding up the other side against it. They apply both approaches to high culture – attacking it either by championing true complexity and artistic aspiration (long since absent in levelled-out bourgeois mass high culture), or by infusing bourgeois culture with the opposite of itself: introducing high-speed styles of entertainment borrowed from mass culture and popular culture, as exemplified in pop art, *nouvelle vague* cinema and in the physical immediacy of experimental theatre.

Each of these four approaches contributed to the construction of countercultures and cultures of division that emerged over the following decades, instigated or underpinned by pop music, most visibly in descriptions and self-descriptions of the new milieu. Each approach, however, contains the familiar paradox of all secessions: I justify my own (specific) deviation in terms of the general (universal) good, which I claim to perceive and understand better than the majority – who are either blinded, backward, docile or even disingenuously attempting to obfuscate the truth. A few years before pop music first emerged in the form of rock 'n' roll, the beatnik movement produced its most famous manifesto (and its most pertinent to pop music-related secessions): Allen Ginsberg's 'Howl'. The poem perfectly illustrates the whole paradox of this model of counterculture: we are the true 'best minds of a generation' – but because nobody understands us, we must segregate ourselves and form an elite (and initiation into this elite means self-destruction).

Connections and disconnections

Though fungible, adaptable and combinable by nature, linking and sub-reception could be condensed, especially into 'movements' like hippie and punk, and thus explained to the majority as meaningful (though not necessarily welcome) phenomena. However, segments of the pop music complex were constantly becoming self-sufficient. Pop music integrated new elements only as quickly as it disintegrated and regurgitated them. Each instance replicated in miniature the mechanics of secession and its paradoxes: each band that broke up for 'musical reasons' followed the same pattern. Since reception is chronologically disconnected and open-ended, pop music recipients continue to generate new and distinct connections as the times move on. Recipients connect with newly offered subproducts that may vary in content and style, but that target the same person or group – with each individual subproduct inviting a new connection. This applies equally to clothing as it does to flawless dance moves, to the stoned demeanour of blokey slackers in the 1970s and of energetically re-masculinized hip-hop fans in the late '80s and early '90s. The singular astonishment that gripped the world when we saw that the mob of far-right Americans whipped up by Trump to storm the Capitol in January 2022 looked much like countercultural tribes of the 1960s and '70s – with one especially obnoxious member dressed almost identically to Larry Byrom from Steppenwolf around 1970 – shows that if we think in terms of single artistic units (music, for example), we overlook the relative autonomy of individual cultural components within the pop music complex. A buckskin-fringed waistcoat, an unshaven look, or certain masculine hip flexes can be lifted from the pop music complex and evolve or grow into new contexts. The fact that they are at all capable of such autonomy (relatively speaking) is because in the pop music complex the next object of sub-reception provides a use value targeted by the previous one. I listen to a bassline at home that provokes me to put on a particular pair of trousers, and these trousers then grant me access to certain cliques in clubs or street corners or schoolyards, and the jargon I learn there equips me for verbal confrontation with older generations or the authorities. From the mid-1950s, pop music users found that – unlike advertising and consumer culture, which had opened up to young people for the first time – pop music commodities, its associated cultural commodities and its noncommodified offerings had, or appeared to have, use values. They seemed to retain their use value regardless of origin and even when their origins had long been forgotten. In Western Europe in the mid-1970s, for example, long hair on men still meant femininity, sensitivity and left-wing or spiritual inclinations, while in the USA as early as 1970 it was associated in some contexts with southern rock and Republicanism.

Autonomization

In Western culture, this process was preceded by a gradual aesthetic appreciation in the value of detachment from artistic interaction and interconnection. In religious and secular contexts alike, events, proceedings, rituals and celebrations historically featured music and dance, an audience to be performed for and involved, and costumes and scenery to depict social complexity. Over several centuries, music was separated from dance, the rise of the First Viennese School heralded the end of table music, the nineteenth century spawned the notion of absolute music, and lyric verse poetry split from music as writing, print books and musical scores became the dominant media. There were key media-historical reasons for this process, but also sound aesthetic ones. By segregating and autonomizing themselves, individual art forms could gain independence from constant censorship via simplification, instrumentalization and circumstantial necessity, while also making space for inutility and prodigality as visions of utopia in a dissatisfying present. This, however, also created the conditions for forms of art that were nothing but distant, antisocial and often vacuously elitist. Nineteenth-century movements and endeavours to reintegrate the arts (the *Gesamtkunstwerk*, for example) anticipated, in their aspirations and principles, what a short time later was made not just possible but standard by technology: the fusion of the arts in cinema, which subsequently facilitated the development of culture industries. Artists' work was taken over by these specialized capitalist industries, though they continued to play out their own self-image as sovereign creative artists. This freed up a now increasingly autonomous space for a fiercely autonomist modernism in poetry and painting, some varieties of which were in theory legitimately anti-industrial and anti-capitalist. One extreme of such autonomization, via the intermediary step of high modernity's aesthetic philosophy of normative media specificity (Greenberg, Adorno, etc.), was conceptual and later postconceptual art – epochal intermediary states that developed through various forms of segregation from, and false reconciliation with, the culture industry, culminating in art that does not have to be realized, or that has to be realized although it does not have to be realized. In the four-part matrix conceived by Henry Flynt in 1963 as a counter-manifesto to the modernist Darmstadt School of new music, one possible option to usher in a new phase of Western culture was 'concept art', i.e., complexity undistracted by its own realization; the other three were African music, African American R&B (i.e., a form of pop music) and minimalist drones.[10] All four supposedly have a use value in common: use values in this instance are bound up with the political, spiritual and social impact inherent within the social organization of the music itself – a construction similar to the (sometimes productive, more often ideological) authenticist confusion

81

of sound recording's indexical objectivity with the ethical or aesthetic sincerity of the recorded person. On the eve of pop music's breakthrough and its subsequent collaboration with the avant-garde (Flynt himself filled in on one occasion with Velvet Underground), Flynt stepped up with this strikingly logical intervention. But in pop music, use values are often linked to another plane: however exhilarating and electrifying this may be, it is all too easy, as we have seen, to dismantle such use values and transform them into Taylorist lifestyle tools.

5

Minus Music: Popularity and Criticism

Four negations of music

The chief mission of this book is to separate the concept of pop music from the concept of music. First for the sake of cultural and historical interest, and second because it might aid our understanding of later, newer cultural complexes that are continually misunderstood by their users and contemporaries, as a result of being metonymically reduced to a single surface feature or element and labelled accordingly. This is not an attempt to praise, celebrate, demonize or condemn pop music for this. Pop music's aesthetic attractions, as should be clear by now, have a number of predecessors; and it only comes into existence through its reception, giving rise to a new type of cultural complex in the second half of the twentieth century. Its production methods are novel too – though it is possible, as we shall see, to pin down a few rules. The question remains whether it is a counterintuitive step – in an art form in which music cannot be disregarded and sound is crucial – to fixate on disavowing or minimizing pop music's connection to music. But we must also consider certain polemics, critiques and corrections of Western musical ideology, which surfaced for various reasons and from various directions over the twentieth century, in relation to pop music and the culture industry underpinning it. The twentieth century in music is characterized by a sense of unease towards the vast Eurocentric affective power ingrained in the functional harmonic system – and in its institutionalized aesthetics. In the twentieth century, we can identify the following specific negations (some of which have been partially discussed already) that were underlined or unleashed by the triumph of recording; they became the forerunners and foundations of the pop music complex:

84

1. Ethnography

The surplus of seemingly unplanned (i.e., unpractised and unscored) elements in recordings can be understood in the context of recording foreignness and foreign traditions. Western-conditioned listeners will reliably ascribe a cultural otherness to the source of unplanned and contingent sound. But this also opens the door to pop music adopting a sonic pose, offering itself for ethnographic study – dressing itself up and presenting itself as the object of ethnographic projections. From the perspective of the Western music tradition, in which scores must be rehearsed, the quasi-ethnographic or ethnographicizable aspect of recordings is a negation of music.

2. Magic and symbolism

Recorded sound – especially sound produced in the studio with the aid of multitrack recording and electronic effects – is always magic sound. Events that cannot instantly be traced to sound sources penetrate sound worlds chiefly characterized by conventional voices or timbres. This is recording's magic: it conjures things up out of nowhere. This is especially effective – even if we know how such sounds were technically produced – when they are heard alongside sounds made by traditional means. Magic is a negation of artistry and ability: a classic negation of the Protestant work ethic. But once such magical (e.g., electronic or otherwise novel and dislocated) sounds are familiar and established, they become symbolic. They come to represent a style, a genre, an artist, or often certain subcultural attitudes and ideas: an electric piano from the '70s, a wah-wah pedal, an 808 are – wherever they are played – pretty much fixed ideologically coded sound sources. This is another crime against music, insofar as sounds become denotative: one of the dogmas of Western (especially so-called absolute) music is that music never consists of unequivocal signs.

3. Star cult as body cult

Diva worship towards the end of the nineteenth century was already at the queer margins of the cult of genius or virtuosity. Female singers were no longer worshipped for their abilities alone, but also for involuntary components of their physicality. In the twentieth century, the rise of the star cult pushed this further: though constantly tempered by auratizing lighting and camerawork tricks, the star's physicality was thrust into the realm of the divine. It was only in the second half of the century (most notably in pop music) that physicality, with all its involuntary aspects, took centre stage. The stage-management of the involuntary remains a contradiction, technically speaking. The reception of stars in pop music, however, is built upon the possibility that we might one day witness live a body that we already know from media transmission – and when we do, we swoon. Being overawed like this is yet another negation of the notions of ability and intention upon which music appreciation normally rests. Their negation occurs not only in this melodramatic form familiar to us since the early '60s (especially later with the rise of boy-bands). Listening to and recognizing a singing, music-making, posing person has for decades been a precondition of pop music's ordinary existence: only at its margins do we find people known only or primarily for live performances, who thus lose the aura of the other mode of existence.

4. Chance, accident, slapstick and small sounds
Fans of Glenn Gould and Oscar Peterson have
always loved the sound of the pianist breathing
and sometimes even grunting or singing along.
In pop music, such effects have become part of
the genre, together with other 'small sounds'
(Cage) that are not exhibited, but embedded
in the recording. Beyond real-world interfer-
ences, quotations and radio-like mashups (the
latter especially in hip-hop), small sounds
appear in the fabric of pop-music recordings
– not just sporadically, but sometimes as constant features of a song, as in 'The Lear Jet Song'
by the Byrds. Unusual small sounds are often
set to beats, as in Lee Perry's music. But more
importantly, when a sound becomes a 'small
sound', it loses the symbolic quality that a once
new, now recognizable noise/sound possesses;
the recipient gets used to hearing it. This strategy of desemanticization and desemiotization
thus points the recipient back towards the real
world: think of noise interference and defamiliarization in the industrial music genre or
later in forms of ambient music, which trace
symbolism-laden sounds back to their original
sources.

88

Pop music and the popular

However, if we separate pop music from music, this invites the question whether the other half of the term – pop – has also lost its meaning through the synthesis of the two. 'Pop' is understood first as an abbreviation of 'popular', and second as a means of describing the workings of pop music and other disciplines with the same prefix, via an onomatopoeic word that the king of British pop art Eduardo Paolozzi emblazoned on a painting as early as the 1940s: 'POP!'. Paolozzi perhaps correctly anticipated the indexical real-world shock value of pop music (he later taught art in Hamburg to original Beatle Stuart Sutcliffe). I have so far underplayed my understanding of the 'popular', not least to counter the widespread preconception that pop music is just another way of saying popular music. But the popular – although no popular music is needed to make pop music – is still an important element of the pop music complex, arising from a cultural-industrial setup that seeks amongst other things to re-implement and re-intensify connections to mass culture and popular culture.

89

In cultural terms, anything that is addressed to everyone assumes the form of the popular. This is one possible definition. Pop music, however, begins with the denunciation of universal communities, via the means by which such communities tend to establish themselves symbolically: through sounds, insignias, performances and codes of conduct. Unlike the elite, with their self-segregating high culture, pop music breaks away from popular culture on popular culture's own turf and by its own means. It announces its secession to others by attacking them either as old, fascist and provincial or as weak, soft and inconsistent. Pop music introduced – first through rock 'n' roll – the possibility of nonconformity into a culture whose foundations and means of representation were built upon conformity and compliance. It did so in the middle of an era (the 1950s) that attempted to teach, preach and enforce conformism: pop music fought back not only against the imperative that a shirt should be white and only a specific brand of cigarette should be smoked, but also, little by little, against all the values championed by the conformists. Pop music succeeded not least because at other levels of capitalism in the late '50s, individuality and deviancy prevailed as a value, tool and product in a high-productivity economy of adjusted subordinates – but also as a norm in management and so-called corporate culture. Vitality and personality were no longer disruptive as they had been in the Fordist days of rock 'n' roll, but their exploitation instead became neoliberalism's essential business model – from dancing Amazon delivery drivers to eccentric waiters.

Pop music presents opposition to historical conformism by harnessing individualism, but also by depicting an alternative collectivism (primarily) through languages and images that serve to articulate compliance. Its songs are comprehensible and rhythmically clear-cut. Despite pop music's constant push for self-determination, it never quite breaks free of this: it is fundamentally affirmative. Pop music says yes. And yet it wants to say no. *I can't get no. It ain't me.* This no, which it conveys to its audience as a yes, is one of pop music's great strengths – a powerful ferment of political mobilization. If its message gets across. It is a joyful – and therefore uplifting and friendly – negation of the status quo in favour of the state its listeners and dancers are in. These two constantly competing descriptions of pop music, a great big happy yes and a great big sardonic no – especially at heroic counter-cultural moments in soul and hip-hop, rave and punk – form a single entity: a no in the form of a yes, and vice versa. It would be inadequate if this refusal were not intrinsically linked to partying, to vast escapist excesses beyond space and time, not unaverse to the ugliness of daily life. But this dialectic core is also a weakness, an Achilles heel: the relationship can be easily and imperceptibly reversed; the respective functions of yes and no are ingrained in the genre, rather than emerging from the evaluation of individual objects.

Historically, pop music as negation means sep-arating those who listen to it and take it seriously from those who do not, amid the great consensus of Fordist class compromise in postwar Western societies. It thus embodies the re-entry of the class divide and the rift between popular and elite within the expanded field of the popular. A 1965 British mod is a form of labour aristocrat that Marx could never have imagined. There is now a distinction, like that between high and low art, within low art and mass culture; it also appears on the other side of the divide, within high art (see pop art) – in each instance with the claim of greater relevance to the times, with an air of greater modernity: a reform of sorts.

But there are other ways of connecting the popular to pop music. Borrowing from British cultural studies, let us say that the popular primarily concerns not what pertains to everyone, but what pertains to the non-rulers. If there is a ruling class whose (homogeneous) culture is distinguished by the fact that it is not enforced, not immediately derivable, and thus functions with relative autonomy, then the popular is its non-autonomous opposite, characterized by necessity (the reproduction of labour power, etc.). Pop music would then be – concurrent with the increasing culturalization of dependent labour – the transformation of this into performance, a display of taste and education down to and dependent on the lowest ranks of the service industry: a kind of autonomous culture of non-rulers (unlike the typical heteronomous cultures of non-rulers issuing from the culture industry and from ideologically motivated state apparatuses). Just like the rulers' high art, it offers utopian visions, moments, and entrance points into a world of noncoercion, but one that is now very different from that of the rulers – especially as coercion is now entangled with self-realization. It is then apprehended and transformed not only by the exploitation of the now culturalized lower classes – utopian laziness becomes reproductive leisure, then assumed cultural self-assurance in industries like gastronomy, the service industry and the creative sector – but also by the restructuring of the bourgeoisie and the middle classes. For where these once based their somewhat homogeneous cultural self-image on cultural knowledge and its affiliated institutions, as members of a regionally and nationally defined cultural class, they are now replaced by new globally active, culturally hybrid upper classes that determine their cultural affiliation no longer through tradition and origin, but through identification and desire.

A third and especially widespread conception of the popular sees it as anything pertaining to new people (in the sense of being new, novel or newly admitted to society) or new things (novelty being their chief characteristic). If the popular is demarcated against the traditional, then the popular is always associated with the ideas of trend and development, because the traditional is the ex-popular, now decaying and consigned to history. Pop music, as the popular culture of young

people and minorities, initially emerges as a representation of the new, but perpetuates its forms
to establish an enduring authority comparable to
that of news broadcasts. In pop music, certain
historical forms of social novelty (new ways of
life or newly admitted agents: migrants, young
people, sexual minorities, women) have con-
gealed into traditions that have not only lost their
original legitimacy, but also won over the (not
only) Western social mainstream. In pop music,
novelty has over time become a value increasingly
detached from the interests of genuinely 'new'
people; it has clung on in the form of value orientation, or has taken on a life of its own. Wherever
its value is still needed for whatever reason, it can
still be deployed in support. Equally, there are
still new experiences had by migrants or digital
natives, for whom pop music remains relevant as
the sound of the new.

With this in mind, we can also introduce a
fourth conception of the popular, to which pop
music again relates in a particular way: the popular pertains to shared sociocultural destinies. It
is the cultural rendering of *shared* experiences,
which are, however, *specific* experiences in the
context of the environment where those affected

by such experiences live. As soon as they address the social majority, their inwardly popular music is no longer popular, but in a sense individual. Pop music, however, is often the result of an unresolved tension between unification and separation, between the shared and the specific. So, when common experiences are shared by (for example) women of African origin in Germany, or Uighur workers living under Han Chinese hegemony, the emergent culture can be called popular if it addresses their shared experiences; but it takes on a different character as soon as it addresses the surrounding social majority in a self-segregating or all-inclusive manner.

One final possible definition of the popular can be found in the enduring critical position that sees industrially produced mass cultures as manipulative and deceitful: i.e., what is presented as entertainment or even liberation actually enslaves in reality. In today's intellectual circles, scepticism towards the internet is reviving many of these ideas in a growing campaign against techno-consumerism. In the age of standardized industrial formats, the popular was conceivable only as a myth. Relative to the ravaged symbols and components of this broken popular culture, pop music represented a fresh start, beginning anew, using the rubble and ruins of a music and language emptied of meaning – charging simple chords, rhythms and schemata with physicality, provoking a shudder through direct transmission of voices, refilling what had been emptied by the manipulative culture industry. In the age of metadata harvesting, we have what looks to be a different problem: it is no longer the symbols themselves that are ruined, but the social formats of participation, of coming together, of assembled diversity – which are the very foundation of consumer data and consumer preferences so crucial to today's society. Here too, though, a reimagined fresh start is not inconceivable. Pop music has undoubtedly represented a kind of avant-garde in today's capitalistic norms of participation, with participation becoming the new spectacle; one of its current endeavours, if we still believe in its potential, is a kind of 'camp' of cheerful bad humour – an updating of what Marcuse called the 'great refusal'. Hip-hop has already laid much of the groundwork for this.

Politics and pop music:
the age of manned space travel

All the constellations in which I have described pop music's relationship to the popular have the following in common: the popular involves stasis, while pop music means dynamism and historical freshness. Pop music emerged in the mid-1950s. But if it represented a new network of connections, we must ask not only what type of music preceded it – what music it developed out of, and which of its extremely diverse styles, from funk to punk, barbershop to narcissistic folk, disco to grindcore, girl-group soul to free improv, can claim to have emerged from this – but also which other connections preceded it; whether perhaps this moment of reinvention and upheaval was not in fact limited to the specific historical transformation of radio music into teenage record music, from radio music to television and image-assisted music; perhaps there were other transformations taking place, turning narrow media-based cultural formats into more complex ones, following a similar pattern to the development of pop music and its consequent forms. Antecedents can of course be found in jazz and other African Diasporic forms: here, too, we find a composite genre of various performative positions (the collective as power, as protection, as exchange, discipline versus individualism, breakaway, escape, self-assertion), a distinct ontology of musical and other sonic signs (derived from various traditions and interpretative practices: pure sound versus musicalization, prosaic versus existential, architectonic construction versus non-teleological music), though given the sheer size of this cultural complex, we can only scratch the surface here. Historically, however, jazz has always benefited from juxtaposing mutually unfamiliar sound worlds and reflecting these unacquainted elements as internal artistic differences, e.g. the difference between sounds that function like acts of speech and sounds oriented in notions of absolute music – but above all those that function as a negation of both, freeing up a new requisite space for communication. Comparable processes can frequently be observed in pop music: negation and refusal as the source of richness, as counterculture in the true sense of the word. A constant feature of jazz is the dramatization, through quasi-speech acts, of balance shifts between individual salvation and collective discipline (and its opposite: collective salvation versus individual downfall) in musically describable terms (solo, tutti) that cannot, however, be reduced to music alone; this makes the unavailable available in a way that is both modern and anti-modern, but that is also closely connected to the specific African American experience. This is transformed into pop music only through the addition of a second experience of foreignness and defamiliarization: the culture-industrialization of large parts of jazz, and the new structure of the second culture industry.

My chosen definition of pop music neatly aligns with the historical period that is most convenient for me to survey – spanning from my year of birth (1957) to (depending on interpretation) the present day, or the establishment of the Web 2.0. This could be construed as vanity or laziness on my part. But perhaps this really is a historically self-contained period. We might call it the age of manned space travel in the USA – the era of NASA astronauts that shares its dates with pop music. After all, manned space travel has always attracted keen interest from the pop music world. Why? Space travel represents a peculiar synthesis of laboratory study and adventure: it is the final incarnation of the idea that knowledge acquisition and scientific observation require first-hand experience, a human participation that also involves existential threat. In pop music, the human participants (artist and recipient) are more important than the work and more impor-tant than the discipline – while faith in control, intention and activity recedes in favour of pose, exposure and letting things happen. The peculiar dislocated human element still taking centre stage is, in both cases, a sort of charming anachronism or even a gesture of embarrassment. Now that we have devices that can measure everything back to the big bang, what need is there for people to witness what is being measured? Now that we can record any old sound, why do we need specialists to produce it? The answer is that we need their affectivity, their physicality, to witness it in the form of experience. It remains an open question whether this is ridiculous, progressive or some-thing else entirely.

The age-old dispute as to whether we can do justice to pop music only through first-hand expe-rience, or only from a critically distanced social and functional theoretical perspective, is equally difficult to resolve. Pop music appreciation

entails the acceptance of its offers of identification and distinction as one's own personal truth
– which simultaneously represents an objective
step towards social integration (or dis-integration
or, much more rarely, integration into something
explicitly different, an 'other society'). As a result,
we can do pop music justice only by illuminat-
ing its transformational character from both
sides, by depicting the subjective wish to belong
and the reluctance to participate, as well as the
responses of the market, state and institutions to
both – but first and foremost, by exploring the
very public route between these two poles. If pop
music were an art in the classical Western sense of
the word, the dialogue between sociological and
aesthetic perspectives would not need to be inter-
rogated. Pop music as a cultural format is yet to
be discussed in aesthetic terms – but many such
attempts have already been made from sociological angles.

While the crisis of the popular is now represented by the problem of populism – a
neo-traditionalism invoking fictitious 'good
old times' and patriarchal values – pop music
is facing a shared crisis with cultures of criticism, specifically social criticism. The fact that

Table of integrations

Bourgeois culture: subjective experience of an object (art) > through bourgeois conversations about art / a public art space / *feuilleton* (the public sphere of discourse on culture), the individual becomes the spiritual precondition of the basic idea of bourgeois society: equality in and through individual irreducibility.	*Pop music:* subjective experience of objectivized (public) other *people* > 1. self-selected sub-society or proto-society; 2. semi-integration (vestibule of society); 3. dissidence / breakaway.

Pop culture: Mixture of the three forms of pop music integration > integration in a culture of general mobilization, characterized by rapidly changing production and reception of media-transmitted, high-resolution vitality.

criticism was once legitimized either by speaking from a partisan perspective, or by speaking in the name of a universalist ideal, is now held against it as two sides of a blind spot. Partisan perspectives are no longer treated as legitimate: specific historical positions (e.g., the proletariat, the vanguard) are no longer ascribed or credited with universal pre-eminence (as they are in Marxism or even, in a more complex way, in intersectional theories around race, class and gender, which opponents know by the reductive term 'identity politics'); nor is the universalist argument any longer allowed to take sides with specific positions, although specificity is necessarily dialectically bound up with criticism. Such, at least, is the claim of hegemonic political and social philosophies such as systems theory and supposedly non-positional liberalism. In this light, pop music actually represents an advance on what critics are lambasted for. For pop music acts almost fundamentalistically from specific stances that do not generally speak in the name of anything in particular, but despite or perhaps because of this speak with real vehemence. Here, the individual perspective and the unlimited subjectivity bound up with it become a source of legitimation: standing alone and saying 'I' is all that is necessary to declare yourself an outsider of society, of the system.[1] Anyone who considers the concurrence of particularism and universalist assumptions (love, peace, partying) to be precarious must also consider pop music precarious – at least as long as it does not present itself as an aesthetic or artistic position alone. While criticism attempts to open the reasons for its particular positions to debate, for pop music, openness to debate often spells the end of its legitimacy – at least in cases like hip-hop, punk and early rock 'n' roll, where individual perspectives are, or were, emphatically or desolately upheld.[2] Although this has become rarer in the pop music of today, especially in its ever more art-like middle-class iterations like so-called indie rock, pop music has long since been able to compensate for the disappearance of emphatic social criticism. To do this, however, the spaceship must be 'manned'; it cannot retreat to political formalism. The laboratory does not *automatically* give rise to the object as cause and actant. Pop music, as manned culture-industrial research, gave rise – counter to the plans of its (culture-industrial) beneficiaries – to the activity of passivity, to the artist as an object offered up for scrutiny.

6

Production Aesthetics

Music is noise made by a subject; pop music is noises generated when subjects are not subjects

This brings us to production aesthetics: i.e., what enables a body or a sound source to stage-manage, situate and implement itself, thus inviting projection or becoming an actual source of the involuntary. Pop music is, for the most part, a form of indexical art, as we have seen. This means not only that it is (usually) recorded and distributed via indexical media, but also that it follows a very particular aesthetic of causation, which is the opposite of what we might call the aesthetic of the old masters in visual art. A painter also 'causes' their work, but by physically implementing their intentions or plans as a master of their craft. They are a master only to the extent that they execute their plans – and where they do not manage this, their work becomes indexical in our sense of the word, the pop music sense that reveals its sources and their (social, material, contingent and essential) causes. Of course, the Dubuffets, Pollocks, Jorns and Pinot-Gallizios of the twentieth century sought deliberate strategies to abandon plans and intentions – especially in the early years of pop music – but they became caught up in aleatoric and other experimental setups that can be understood as plans of another kind. If we are serious about the idea of an indexical art that is recording-media-specific, post-humanist and anti-subjective in equal measure, this is not enough. But what is the alternative? So far, we have discussed the forerunners of indexical art in funfair aesthetics and ethnography, but the next question is how and when we can get around the paradox – in pop music and its later, often lowlier relatives in internet performances and talent shows – of provoking the involuntary, which is so essential to indexical art, in a targeted and somewhat voluntary way. A first observation is that we know how suitable targeted and intentionally monotonous music (The Fall) or any non-teleological tradition (parts of Africa, India and Pakistan) is for this purpose.

Classical aesthetics presuppose that the arts deal in languages (symbols) and images (icons), while indexical elements are left to media formats and their technical particularities. Pop music, then, is subject to the fundamental rules of all indexical arts or cultural practices, as formulated for photography by Roland Barthes.[1] The photo is an object *caused* by the photographed thing, as a result of its physical presence in a specific light in a specific place: the photo is thus an indexical object whose singularity cannot be put to a specific purpose – i.e., the documentary or artistic aims of the photographer – but is realized in an involuntary singularity, called the 'punctum'. The punctum is a specific detail revealed by the contingency and irretrievability of the moment when the photograph is taken. It is, however, a phenomenon of reception: there is no objective punctum, but multiple possible ones. It presupposes empathy for the affecting, ephemeral, living spark that emerges from a frozen instant. The punctum is contingent by definition and never conforms to intention – neither a formal artistic

intention nor an informative documentary intention. Rather, the punctum is a quasi-metaphysical
zone of pure mediality within photography and
phonography alike. Its focus on involuntary
effects (voice, sound, etc.) is key to the aesthetics
of pop music. Just as pop music makes a socio-
logically impossible claim – that it can connect
the social outside with its inside – it also attempts
the impossible according to Barthes's phenom-
enology of indexical media: it seeks to *control* the
punctum (in a cultural-industrial or artistic or
mixed sense).

We have already seen how the studio serves
the function of the peopled laboratory, and how
what it produces cannot be credited either to
a single mastermind composer or writer as in
classical music, or to a combo collectively negotiating a real-time situation as in jazz – although of
course, like any practice, it plays with its limits,
requiring a variety of different recording situations to bring the game of recognition to life. Pop
music's point of reference is not the composition
(i.e., a written-out plan), nor the mere *recording date* (i.e., documentation of a session in the
studio or on stage), but a recording completed in
the studio together with a producer, inextricably

accompanied by visual packaging (cover, inner sleeves, booklet, etc. – with specific graphics, typography, photos, etc.). In other words, a large number of symbolic and iconic accessories are called on to present authoritatively what in photography would be called the 'studium'. The inflated importance of these non-indexical elements – especially when they appear in media formats different from the recording and the performance – seems to improve the likelihood of involuntary elements (or what we might take to be involuntary elements) occurring; in other words, there is a calculated gap between phonographic 'punctum' reception and the 'studium'[2] of graphic cover design and makeup decisions.

The punctum is never where you want it to be; it always crops up somewhere else.[3] It is not subject to the intentions of artist-subjects communicating in a targeted manner (a familiar problem in pop music); instead, it is dependent on chance and on an empathetic, unsuspecting spectator ready – at the moment when life reveals itself to be mortal – to fall in love. 'Chance is not an aesthetic concept', remarked Pierre Boulez of John Cage's 'Chance Operations'. 'You cannot compose chance.'[4] But even if not, you can open the door to it and pave the way to it – via performance.

Who do you love?

Here's another way of putting it: if there is no centre to the connection and configuration network of pop music apart from recipients' desires and their consummation, and if physicality and specific indexical signals form the only constant, then what exactly is the object of desire? Who or what are you in love with? It is not sexuality or vitality or sentimentality in itself (as, for example, in classic popular music), but the sentimentality and sexuality of a given person – a person (or a small group of people) who is usually shouting, bragging, whispering, crying or playing it cool. It must be a specific person, simultaneously singular and individual and addressable and yet a stranger, in order for us to be not just alone with a projection, but alone with a powerful other. This other is as concrete a person as my friends, but in the endless open space of strangerhood they also represent the many who make up society. In them I find a representative of society, a stranger, but also a confidant, home-delivered to me via irrefutable, fetishizable traces of their physicality and their feelings. Insofar as I can imagine them from the information presented to me by two very different types of sign – indexical sounds and noises attesting to real physicality versus idealized, iconic visuals – this representative becomes somehow real. They not only occupy worlds both real and imaginary (like talkie stars of old), but I actively combine these two planes to construct the person: they belong to *my* reality. The symbolic plane, which engages with both these planes, is my ordinary life.

The agents of pop music are therefore neither plain performers of a role, nor plain speech actors, speaking for themselves as real people. A constitutive aspect of all pop music is that it must not be obvious at any given moment in a performance whether a persona or a real person is speaking. This is a vital rule of the game. The ideology of authenticism – i.e., the attempt to declare non-acting and non-lying as a transcendent virtue, and to judge pop music accordingly – and its closely related opposite, rock theatre, are where pop music (and discourse around it) regularly comes unstuck, perishes, even; in both instances, pop music quickly reaches a tediously absolute limit – which nonetheless is always appealing to play with, and which ultimately helps to reinforce this rule. Authenticism is initially quite understandable: an index does indeed convey authentic traces, and the pop recipient is driven by insatiable curiosity as to the identity of their counterpart, whom they know only as a name, as a myth. What kind of person are they really? How do they come across? What attitude do they give off? What pose do they strike? Anyone who believes that pop music is only as good as its ability to answer these questions satisfactorily is an authenticist and has understood nothing. Pop music is as good as the question or questions that it enables us to ask. All that it authentically transmits is a signal that is meaningless in itself; the task is to connect this signal, in a way that is neither obvious and realistic nor fantastical and imaginary, with images, narratives and, above all, musical (i.e., never denotative) and sonic (i.e., usually real-world-sourced) elements. This does not work, however, without a key ingredient of pop music production: the pose. The pose amounts to the skills and techniques of offering oneself up for projection, for a punctum experience, opening oneself to a searching, rapt gaze without forcing it – without becoming active. This works best when people are absorbed or seem absorbed by something that hooks them but that is neither expressive (i.e., revealing anything) nor performative (demonstrating or asserting anything). A perfect example is playing rhythm guitar, bass or drums. Think of The Fall, or Can. Or Bo Diddley.

This, like all the characteristics of pop music that I am assembling here, is not a ploy, nor a question of success; it is not an artistic goal of individual performers, but an unspoken rule of the game, without which what we call pop music does not work. Its rules mark pop music out from other cultural formats, though these other formats have also fed certain modifications into it, increasingly so over recent decades. Such formats fall under the much-discussed title of pop *culture* – not music, but systems founded on the same rules governing pop music: consider YouTubers, Insta-influencers and TikTok celebrities. They naturally raise the question whether music's involvement has not been vital in preserving something about the aesthetics of the performative in-between.

Performance and pose

Substituting reception aesthetics for production aesthetics, perhaps the star performer and their tool, the pose, is the centre of every pop-music 'work' in production terms. This is implied by the fact that how a person looks (what is their mission, their game, what kind of person are they?), when we have only ever *heard* them before, is the first thing we want to know; and thirst for knowledge is what defines the entirety of pop music reception. Recipient behaviour involves a persistent search for the essence, the origin, the actuality of the star (note that 'star' means not necessarily a superstar, but anyone worthy of veneration, from low-key indie legends to trashy one-hit wonders to Beyoncé). This centrality, however, is not the stable centrality of the old authorial function, but a new, fleeting centrality that must be created anew as a side-effect of any 'product': an 'I'-single.

If I worship Sarah Bernhardt based on a single postcard, she *is* the image on the postcard. She has no other form of life and no other ontology (at best a completely fantastical one that I can develop by myself as far as I like). The star whose image I come across repeatedly – a different image in different circumstances each time – becomes a portentous substance, solidifying into the suggestion of a self beneath the surface, beneath all these images. This being has simultaneously more and less substance than the old saints who we know from one picture or one characteristic pose. The star is limited by the clear, unambiguous evidence of their voice and instruments, by their distinct and yet enigmatic signals – and by my fascinated imagination that interprets this flood of images and finds constant similarities between them. The star is, however, not an invention, but a constantly changing outcome – a series of temporary states that have endless new repercussions on the recipient's sacralizing abstraction.

This chain of identifications, this mutating and multiplying face can also be found in the average Hollywood star. In their case, as an actor, it is part of their job to transform themself. Pinning down the identity of the mutable actor is one of the oldest games in theatre; the game is intensified and catalysed – though not fundamentally transformed – by film and film publicity, typecasting and public image. In the final analysis, however, the actor is an institution that does not dissolve identity and authenticity, but confirms it. At the end of the day, the actor sits in their dressing room and cracks jokes about stage fright. The actor is firmly themself: their every transformation has an end point. This mercy is not afforded to the pop musician. For them, there is no stable place unaffected by their fictitious existence. When the pop star is alone at the end of the day, unlike the actor, they are not niggled by faint afterpains of their day's work on stage; instead, this is the precise moment – alone, away from their job, away from dissembling – when they are meant to be writing new intimate songs about their own life, that they will then perform to their audience over the coming year. The pop star operates in a constant grey area between 'expression' and 'performativity'. The fan dissolves this in the search for a higher being, or for a fluid product behind the paradox. And the paradoxical system is confirmed by the fact that the best way to negotiate a paradox is to construct a higher being. A god is more widely applicable, and mobilizes more people more intensely than a mere saint, who – as usually happened to old-school stars – is typecast, limited to a single function.

In classical performance – be it in theatre or in a musical show – conscious adulation of technical ability and illusionistic entrancement are systematically located at *one* point in the performance. The performance's strategy of legitimation is to provoke the concurrent and interconnected reception experiences of outstanding craftsmanship (which I can comprehend) and simultaneous amazement (which I cannot comprehend). But entertainment forms predating pop music were geared towards more than just a perfect performance unrelated to the world outside. The goal was to create tension between the inevitably imperfect but at times overwhelming aspects of the performance and its relevance to something beyond the concert hall (not just literary or topical references: text, performance history, etc.). Pop music performance also exists in a state of tension, not least with filmed performances of the same stars (be they performances at the artistic end of the scale – appearances in feature films, e.g. *Fun in Acapulco* – or at the 'authentic' end of the scale, through naturalistically filmed real-life appearances in direct cinema documentaries). But what really sets pop music apart is how it utilizes the speech act – of personally addressing the audience – as contrasted with ritualized inter-missions in other performance cultures. In pop music, directly addressing the audience no longer serves a de-intensifying, distancing or ironizing function. In fact, it is precisely the opposite: it is a moment of intensification. This is an essential component of its live formats. The statements that the performer makes during the speech act are more explosive than the artistically designated part of their performance.

Interruption and disunity

Pop music performances live off the tension between the relative perfection of a live recon-struction of a perfect studio recording, on the one hand, and radical deviation from it, on the other. In referencing the studio recording, the performance works with the charm and the eroti-cism of its own inadequacy, pointing to the living presence of the star on stage (ostensibly much more in command of intention and causation); but its main point of reference, the stronger pole, is the (ostensibly less controlled physicality of the) studio recording, which it can be assumed the audience know already. Deviant improvised or accidental parts of the performance, however, point not towards the studio recording – to what authenticists snidely call canned music – but towards the portentous personality behind it all, the essence of the star, the (fluid) entity bestowed with a higher ontic status: God rather than saint. Their joint presence is the foundation of intensification through interruption.

Jimi Hendrix was one of the first to master the use of short evocative phrases to break the barrier between saint and God on stage. Hendrix always seemed erratic, pausing, coughing and changing subject. But if we examine his various comparable comments on 'Machine Gun',[5] we can reconstruct how even 'ahs' and uncertainties in his compèring were planned in detail – perhaps even actual stage routines. Only authenticists will be disappointed by this. 'Yeah – ah – groovy – yeah – ah – out of sight, man.' Hendrix talks hipster slang. He draws out the beginning of his version of Dylan's 'Like a Rolling Stone' for an eternity, presenting the song as a protracted prelude to the real firecrackers – an unending display of pure, sheer coolness, without cause or beginning or end. Coolness as delay, as a pose that keeps promising and promising. He wallows in the potentiality of the pose, its declaration of readiness. It is as hot as the intensity of his noise and feedback passages elsewhere, the ultimate extreme of improvisation: at their climax, the performance surrenders to physical effects, passing the torch to pure electricity.

Like so many structures, the simultaneous presence of saints, God and ordinary servants and instrumentalists in pop performance can be traced back to traditions from African American (and African Diasporic) cultures – particularly in terms of managing the difference between ritual constants and individual variables in a performance. Forerunners can be found in the typical Afro-Baptist church service, but also in some other – especially syncretic – liturgies and rituals. Here, it is the priest who acts as a 'compère', interrupting and 'moderating' the songs of the choir and community, and thus intensifying rather than de-intensifying them. Such interruptions signify not the controlledness of the event (as conventionally promised by compères at ordinary shows), but rather an incitement to lose control. The speech act, which calls personally upon individual members of the community and their 'testifying' – as they ecstatically bear witness to God taking possession of them – does not interrupt the escalation in momentum and intensity that underlies the dramaturgy of the service. The change in reference points between God and those present – between their bodies, where religious ecstasy is taking hold, and their worldly names; toing and froing between these spaces, from this church here and now with these bodies that right here and right now are being seized by God and the Holy Spirit, to a distant, unfathomable deity – if all this happened in a Wagner opera or a Kubrick film, it would be an inexcusable breach of a painstakingly constructed atmosphere. In this case it not only is not that, but it actually escalates the atmosphere.

White exoticism and its accompanying projections, and also some forms of Afrocentrism, claim that Black or African American culture is based in a more unified corporeality, oblivious to the strict distinction between spirituality and sexuality on which European culture is founded. As far as I can see, the opposite is true, and the former aspires much less to completeness and unity than the European *Gesamtkunstwerk* and similar formats of consolation and reunification. In some genres of African American culture, we find sudden shifts in points of reference, which are seen by audiences and participants not as a distracting interruption of the illusion (not least because they are not dealing in illusion), but as the manifest point where the audience and preacher envision interaction – or, less prosaically, fusion. This fusion, however, is not the effect of a unified social fabric. The entities to be unified are two, or become two amid mounting ecstasy. Call *and* response, God or spirituality *and* the self. Intensity is found not in the singular, but in the plural. One person steps forward and howls, speaks in tongues (a sound much like the typical Albert Ayler saxophone solo), the possessed person sings their song, bears witness, lets the spirit possessing them run riot – surrounded all the time by an audience that will supply the next soloist a moment later.

This structure, which lingers on in jazz combos and hip-hop posses, functions in performance terms only to the extent that audience members genuinely feel themselves to be potential participants. This has gradually been restored in hip-hop shows and battles; it was previously the principle of the jam session in jazz. In pop music concerts, however, potential audience participation is often subdued into the dullest rituals. The audience can at best be brought to life in commodity form, which has already divided those present into two groups: the desiring and the desired, the paying and the paid. Attempts to uncage desire consistently mark concerts out as the beginning of a movement: hippie '66, punk '77, rave '88. It is the moment when participants' self-image craves an immediacy that the concert structure cannot offer. It is then that laconically transgressive interaction with the compère becomes an intensifying force, as with Jimi Hendrix. But even in classic teenage pop concerts, where audience and performers have clearly distinguished roles, the sudden loudness of the speaking voice perforates the spectacle of the melody. *It's me*, it says, just as the singing voice says the opposite. Both, of course, do this only by allusion; teenagers cannot handle the whole truth.

Camp and the ontology of stardom

Images have a part to play on both sides of a staged performance. First, they are responsible for spectacular production effects and for the moment of identification, the outburst of *It's me!*

or *There he is!* and for the subsequent camera shots of young people that hold up a mirror to other young people, facilitating their pop socialization. The most reliable way of learning about sound–image relations is when you are young, playing air guitar or singing into a pretend microphone in front of the mirror, where you will also learn to put makeup on. Ultimately, however, images also play a part in our enjoyment of a performance and its production beyond the straightforward *It's me!* and *There he is!* There are two questions about voice to be addressed here: first, we might ask what brought about the hegemony of weakness and weak voices in pop music; second, we might ask whether this sexiness formula – i.e., revealing weaknesses in the voice and exposing the indexicality and contingency of transmission and recording – can be considered a vocal attribute. If our enjoyment of a singer's pose is so closely connected to the voice, and if the voice's quality, which perforates its creation of meaning, forges an enigmatic indexical connection with the secret (godlike) personality of the singer, then it is difficult to conceive how any visible, visual performance would not end in disappointment. How can a physically present person ever satisfy the promise that their voice once made – especially when that promise has been made in the manner of a voice from the dead, promising contact with another reality: the ontology of the star?

Body language and staging in performance must take this factor into consideration. A triumphant climax to the evening, as in the shows of strong singers like Little Richard and conventional pre-pop greats, is out of the question. Stars in the mould of Dylan, Hendrix, Curtis Mayfield or Neil Young – and their millions of descendants in indie rock, soul and singer-songwriter culture up to the present day – have to emerge slowly and apparently passively out of the stage structure. The *There he is!* effect must come from a sense of wonder that slowly builds to certainty. Perhaps it can be kept open for a while longer. Perhaps a doppelgänger has been sent out on stage. But it is perhaps even better to remain an image only, never appearing on stage, since commanding the stage always has something to do with power, with performances of masculine charisma. So the performer does not step forward, but reveals themselves only when the spotlight falls on them by chance.

But how can we get close to stars in visual images that – unlike the *voice*, which is much better suited to metaphysics – religions like to condemn as inappropriate? Images are also the gateway to the 'emancipated' reception culture known as camp aesthetics. This specializes primarily in visual documentation and photographs of Hollywood stars and other celebrities who are meticulously presented, with nothing in their presentation left to sacred chance. Fans of camp accept the invitation to fetishism, if we can call it fetishism, in which individual visual moments – 'Look how she holds that cigarette!' – are singled out and elevated. This is something different from a love of contingency, but the two are neighbours: both styles of reception respond to an allure that appears only at the edge of (or as a metonym for) the intended meaning of the cultural object.

Camp theorists like Philip Core[6] work with the theory of the open secret. Appreciation of camp is based on things (or details) pointing towards a truth about a particular star that is otherwise hidden from view and excluded from official narratives – in most cases, this involves a persecuted or inconvenient sexual orientation.

Eve Kosofsky Sedgwick systematizes this hypothesis: camp recipients ask themselves what it would be like if 'whoever made this was gay too? . . . What if the right audience for this were exactly me? What if, for instance, the resistant, oblique, tangential investments of attention and attraction that I am able to bring to this spectacle are actually uncannily responsive to resistant, oblique, tangential investments of the person, or some of the people, who created it?'[7]

In this sense, the viewer's attention shift from fundamental meanings to 'unimportant' fetishized details is not just a subjective response – encouraged by freely offered objects and enigmatic, contingent signs of life – it also finds solid objective and necessary justification in its creator. Of course, this creator cannot always be defined in the sense of 'coming out' within definable criteria – in the process of which a clear distinction is drawn between a hegemonic and an ostracized identity, an opposition that the creator alludes to. It is not about unequivocal, verifiable knowledge; what matters is the opportunity to find evidence that the creator of an object is talking to me, and to those like me: I am moved for more than just my own sake. Visual performances and images of stars constantly function as potential evidence: they enable us to consider for ourselves what in every other medium is only implied. The performance itself is fleeting, but the individual who might provide us with information, who might confirm a suspicion, is personally present, exhibiting themself as a physical being with intentions. The visual image, meanwhile, is patient, allowing itself to be looked at again and again, and at some point, as we know, looking back: 'uncannily responsive', as Eve Kosofsky Sedgwick puts it. It is an answer relayed from another ontology.

Here, then, we have a grid of four related phenomena (see p. 130). The pose is a performance that leaves open what might happen, while also implying a general openness to experience and adventure. The image fixes the pose, crystallizing an iconic entity that forms the reference point for the pose during a performance, but that also limits the possibilities of the pose. The image, meanwhile, invites projection, fetishization, the camp conjecture of the open secret, but also invites us to find a punctum – an open, unintentional and affecting moment stemming from the indexicality of the photo or film reel. Recipients of this type curb the tendency of iconic images to become closed; instead, they open the image to reality, perforating the image. Finally, live performance, despite all the performance of the pose, sees the body moving intentionally in a targeted and possibly choreographed manner; it constantly works towards the pose, but can hardly hold it for any length of time.

Openness, recipient activity	Fixedness, denotation
Idealized performance pose: potentiality, availability to the fan	Widely distributed idealizing images of the star (not only photos, but also poster and logo design): fixing, definition
Image reception (mostly photos or film): openness, punctum, camp, projection	Performance practice: intention, unavailability to the fan

The making of

Punctum and pose work together towards openness, enabling subjective fetishistic projections and the objective disclosure of a secret meant for me. Choreography and staged (i.e., as punctum-free as possible) visuals provide the stable points of reference on which any production depends – and whose predictable and officious nature threatens to kill pop music performances. Roland

Barthes conceives the punctum in photography very plausibly as impervious to intention and art. The punctum is an idiosyncratic detail that exists in tension with, even in contradiction to the wider planned work. Similarly, the pose is constantly threatened by the logic of advancing time and the dramatics of stage appearances (especially musical ones). You could say that pop music is kept alive by a presence at a false media location: there must be someone on stage who looks like a photo – a pose, a living image – and who in the photo looks as if they are performing, communicating something, inviting us in. In both cases, it is recipient activity that helps to manufacture the impossible: the planned punctum, the living image (Warhol's *Screen Tests* were genuine attempts to produce both performing photos and posing acts). Pop history is rich in attempts to manufacture what can only be let happen – what with its permitted mistakes, constant interruptions and delays. But punctum appreciation only makes sense when it is turned against a squeaky-clean commodity aesthetic (which is equally performed or virtually present), not when it consists of nothing but crass mistakes or boyish overkill: unbroken vitality is the natural enemy of both functions. This fine line was trodden very successfully in the 1980s by bands such as The Cramps, who were strong at both performing an act and interrupting it. The hole through which recipients penetrate the tightly sealed profit-driven world of pop superficies cannot be allowed to open too far in a world that is already open. Its mystery and its truth become all the more drastic and seductive the opaquer its surface remains.

In a theory of the photographic pose,[8] Craig Owens sets out valuable arguments as to how we might describe the production of what is manufactured and intended, but received as contingent and accidental, as incidentally beautiful – as a moment that is snatched and seized on. He explains this using a grammatical metaphor. In Ancient Greek verb formation, between the two grammatical voices (active and passive) that we know from most European languages, there is a third: the so-called middle voice. Verb forms in the middle voice are usually translated as reflexive: 'to show oneself' would be the middle-voice infinitive, where in the active it is 'to show' and in the passive 'to be shown'.

The middle form of showing oneself signifies the essential impossibility of deliberately crafting an incidental moment. It is 'practised' chance, it means being caught by calculation – the sudden opening of a door that gives a performance true meaning. The radical joy of unearthing an intrinsic flaw, an indexical truth about the artist, by making a discovery equivalent to the delightful revelations of the punctum, is, on the one hand, a prerequisite for the survival of the pop musician's constitutionally unclear and open status. On the other hand, an effect that is too predictable or too closely controlled destroys it altogether. There is the possibility, as pursued by hippie pop music, of increasing the likelihood of unplanned intensity and surprising discoveries by using open forms: Grateful Dead, some prog rock, Miles Davis, and so on. Countering this is the camp argument that in performances where there are no limits, no restraints and no hint of hermeticism, not only does the crack in the doorframe lose its explosive power, but so does whatever is hiding behind it. Anyone who exhibits themselves fully and confidently the whole time is less true and has less punctum sex appeal than a completely hermetically sealed commodity-like mass-cultural performance, the door to which opens only for a few seconds or perhaps not at all

– but promises to open. Here we can see the old argument between performativity and expressivity rearing its head once more.

Roland Barthes later developed the concept of the neutral,[9] which seems to function as a superordinate to what I have described here as the pose: a third voice between action and passion. It can be extended in principle to an attitude that desires action – especially transgressive and transcendent action – but does not wish to be its initiator. It is about an attitude of permissiveness, of letting things happen; it is about making oneself the object of an action, or just becoming it – without making oneself anything. The dreaming, fantasizing, imagining subject has always been capable of this: it is the heart of ancient, pre-media poetry. In the age of the aesthetics of causation and indexicality, however, pure imagination no longer exists: all images and sounds are caused directly by reality, never just invented or dreamed up; even the dream itself becomes material. This is, in a sense, an adult sexualization of art itself, which was previously juvenile masturbation – a freer activity. Within this new consequentiality (both in the media-based genesis of today's art and in its reception, where likes and clicks register immediately), art must become queer if it wants to avoid becoming either trivial and commodified or violent.

Pop minus music

Today's pop culture (minus or postpop music) imitates both the media specifics and the performative characteristics of pop music, mainly for the purposes of cheap entertainment. Reality shows, hidden camera pranks, but also certain artistic performances since the 2000s and 2010s – and, above all, neo-documentary (Artur Żmijewski, Jeremy Deller, Vanessa Beecroft, Phil Collins, etc.) and interventionist (Thomas Hirschhorn, Santiago Sierra, etc.) artistic styles – work deliberately with the ambiguity of the performer function, cultivating a logic of attraction in which chance, accident and physically instigated singularities (now transmitted rarely through sound, but usually through images, often cheap and digital ones) are merged with idealized images (now by the producers themselves, not by active recipients). Moreover, the activation of recipients as consumers is a central criterion of digital consumption – from constant ratings to digital community building and endless commenting. This suspended state of semi-integration no longer functions primarily as a necessary fiction enabling unintegrated people to construct an outsider perspective into society or a vestibule-of-society illusion (with its corresponding reality of possible life paths kept open for longer). Instead, it has become the normal state of post-Fordist, semi-disintegrated relations.

If a future pop music were to free itself from *pop culture* as I understand it, it could either become straightforward art – or amplify its primal components. If it becomes art (as it often does), it has two options. It can liberate individual components of pop music – e.g., a certain musical style – and push them further in an art-like, self-reflexive and intentional manner (Sunn O)))). Or, more interestingly, it can thematically address the entire complex that constitutes pop music and that has become the model for pop culture, approaching it as a kind of institution-critical meta-pop-music (Terre Thaemlitz).

If it is not seeking to become art, it can continue what techno culture began and many genres, sometimes clustered under monikers like ghettotech, are now trying to push beyond the boundaries of old Western-dominated pop music: it can recalibrate elements of indexical proximity, recognition and public space, visuals, etc. – deleting some elements (the star) and extending others (the transmission of physicality no longer as an individual's physicality, but, re-interpreted symbolically, as collective physicality: beats).

Non-teleological music

There are several (but not an infinite number of) ways to organize musical affect. Western classical music uses an architectonic model. We can always visualize what the whole structure looks like from a distance: its organization is fixed and although it is executed in real time, it retains at all times a firm grasp of its elements and of their finiteness and finality, i.e. their end in a dual sense, as closure and as purpose. It is structured towards an end and its elements are purposeful: they are preparing something, they have a concrete meaning. Its tendency towards absoluteness, towards self-containment, corre-lates to this inner purposefulness. It illustrates perfectly the central notion of Kantian aesthetics:

'purposiveness without purpose'. This model is directed at a recipient who is both emotionally involved and grasps intellectually the meaningfulness of its organization. The process amounts to a twofold endorsement of the European subject as a meaningful construction of rationality and emotionality situated in time. Every sonata is a life of beginning, tension, animation, resolution and ending – including temporary resolutions and temporary endings. It is always conceived as the life of the subject from birth/design to death/result. It is only observed and observable from the outside; the art always consists in shaping the moment while acting in such a logical and rationally aesthetic manner that an informed recipient can keep one eye or one ear on the whole work.

Non-teleological music does not split the subject into observer and observed. Instead, the subject is found in every role within the music. The music – and this applies to much of African and African Diasporic music, though by no means exclusively (Pakistani, Indian and some Indonesian music is often non-teleological, while there is a whole range of African Diasporic music that is not non-teleological) – has no categorical beginning and no categorical end. Weather, light and other forces take care of that. Death is not the end, but the puncture in every syncopated beat; the beat constantly dances around and 'embeds' (my favourite word, not without reason, for the relationship of heterogeneous elements in pop music) the non-presence of the non-beat. Music of this type has no dramaturgy that an outside observer can anticipate or remember. They can only either help shape what is happening in the moment or await certain twists and turns. This music contains a similar range of activities, of combinations of individuals and groups, individuals and individuals, etc. They do not, however, contribute to an overall architecture, but to a mixture of collective diary, saga and series – more rhizome than tree, with many shoots but no bifurcations. Non-teleological music gave pop music not just the back beat (which became the key method of embedding), but also the mode of ordinariness, of seriality, in which pop-music-related events, releases and broadcasts happen – as moments of excess and ecstasy that belong to ordinary life, whose few quasi-climactic manifestations do not occur within individual trajectories.

Aesthetics of causation

Art that works with technological media – especially sound art – always speaks of its causation. It therefore works with tricks and magic, because we often only know *that* something has been caused – not *how*. This was a central attraction when recording practices first emerged, and it has since spilled over into artistic content. The best-loved plot in television entertainment is still the question: Who was the perpetrator? Who caused this? In pop music, however, the question is more complex. There is an obvious perpetrator (or several), who is exhibited via visual and other non-auditory media, and then there are the sounds, which do not always demonstrably have the same source. The body we desire is not (always) that of the creator (if there even is a creator identifiable to non-geeks). This grey area – Who is playing what? Whose voice is that really? Is that what they really look like when they are actually doing that? – is a source of energization. An even greater one, however, is the associated search for intention and responsibility – which is of course implicitly denied or sidelined by the pose. Pop musicians constantly admit in interviews that they do not know how what is attributed to them came about: they dismiss probing questions with the old adage 'My music speaks for itself' – a fundamentally false, at best strategically justifiable, phrase. Questions around pop musicians' unusual manner of causation usually invite the follow-up questions: Has someone created this person? Is there a Svengali figure behind the scenes? This line of questioning is frequently motivated by the often sexist and racist idea that behind any sensational sound there must be some Western authorial mastermind. And searches have often been undertaken. Not least by critics, propelled by the elitist critical conviction that arts of directness, of causation, of noise and of thick makeup are propagated by dark corporations to make the uneducated, oppressed and submissive rabble even stupider and more oppressed.

At a superficial level, there are of course institutions of control and profit maximization lurking behind the structures that enable and variously benefit from the distribution and heterogeneous dissemination of pop music across the world. The pop music constellation connects oppositional energies. Realia, or staged breakthroughs to physical realia (the key to pop music's allure), pertain to the existence of real people and not just to their prosaic learned abilities. While this is in one sense a chink in the armour of the spectacle, nowadays it is to a much greater extent the foundation of the business model of authenticity porn, which reaches far above and beyond pop music.

When people exhibit themselves, reveal things, suggest things and adopt the pose to let something shimmer through, they can only succeed if the aesthetic and institutional framework of this exhibition of vulnerability exceeds mere bedding and scenery. This might necessitate, for instance, the re-musicalization of pop music as a weapon or a powerful tool in the hands of the people revealing themselves. Or it might involve the refinement and enhancement of noise, of machine causation, enabling the queer humanity of the pose to combine with the post-human attractions of causation. Pop music has to keep inventing new aesthetics as its institutions, as the indie label, the club and the festival once were. In this respect, pop music has always been at its most influential at the times when it refused to believe in the capitalistic notion of lost authentic innocence, but instead evolved – by affirming its profanity, its ordinariness and its closeness to sex work – into an aesthetic of solidarity.

Communities and elites

Distinction must be made between positions within pop music aesthetics, in its transient free space. There are two sides to this distinction. On one side is the 'hipster',[10] whose acts of divergence are approved of; on the other side, when they are not approved of, is the 'nerd'. Similarly, an integrated community whose collective outcome is approved of is 'soulful'; if scorned, it is 'mainstream'. If it is considered attractive as a whole, it is 'soulful' in line with the model of the spiritually connected, active recipient community in Afro-Baptist church services that in a sense lives on in rave culture; if it reveals itself to be a capitalistically calculated conformist consumer culture worthy of rejection, it is 'mainstream'. Returning for a moment to systems theory's tried-and-tested arguments, pop music is about organizing non-affiliation and special communication – without falling back on traditions like church services, rituals, the nonconsequential ontology of the art work and so on – opening the question of whether each (provisional) mediation between the whole and particular (the lone individual) is too general or too special, too large or too small. Arguments around this must take into account the fact that the small or large thing in need of correction will get a bad name, and the next largest or next smallest a good name.

As we have seen, the cultures emerging around pop music, or adopted by it, cannot be simply identified in content terms with resistance or dissidence. The formal, systems-theory-inspired depiction of a society – incorporating more and more special communicative connections that cannot be ascribed to classical systems or subsystems – implies that society becomes the object of (radical) criticism only where and when its status is seen in a temporary light. The notion of postponement,[11] which Pierre Bourdieu identified in the 1960s as characteristic of the self-image (or the grand delusion) of many culture workers – the notion that I do things only provisionally, only in parentheses, only for now, because I am really someone else – is more or less perpetuated by the pop music world. The fact that this perspective also stimulates political criticism amongst other things – even if it is consistently rubbished by the mainstream in the same society – reveals pop music subcultures as agents of democracy who, unlike directly impli-cated stakeholders in society, can keep one eye on the whole. Where subcultures fall down is in the misconception that such revolutionary zeal and incorruptibility is a personal quality in them-selves, rather than a construction of the society they live in and observe.

Reporting the event, being the event

The structure of pop music responds to this blind spot with a fundamental division of all its genres into two types – a division that also has conse-quences for its protagonists. On the one hand, there is the model in which the protagonist, the performer, arrives from somewhere else and tells us about it. They have been shaped by an experience, and their pose is a consequence of the gravity of that event or long chain of events. They might be called Leonard Cohen or Curtis Mayfield. They had their experiences somewhere beyond the world where they now appear (the world of direct transmission) – somewhere in a world of succession, of narratives – but now they offload their accumulated wealth of experience in a studio session or a live performance. The audience asks them: 'Where have you been, my blue-eyed son, where have you been, my darling young one?' And he has been in battle, where a hard rain was falling. The other model, meanwhile, is not about reporting on the event that has influenced the body of the messenger, the transmitter – but about attempting to unleash the event here and now. The most common formula for this is the invitation to dance, to let go, to behave differently; there are friendly and aggressive variants of this model. And there are mixtures of both strategies: Jimi Hendrix and Prince spring to mind. Certain genres appear more suited to one or the other model, but what matters more in every style of pop music is that its suitability is never conclusively decided – just as it is never quite decided whether the performer is referring to themself or to their persona, or whether moderating and directly addressing the audience represents an interruption or an intensification. The concept of the male gaze – i.e., the view of women inherent in classic narrative cinema camerawork, depicting women as marked and special, available and object-like, juxtaposed with an unmarked view of men and correspondingly unmarked male actors – has arguably undergone a transformation in pop music scenarios. The classic patriarchal demarcation of the masculine has been superseded in pop music by a mystery that sums up the pop music experience: Where has the star come from? Are they now absolutely here, or are they still connected to an outside world of some sort? Is it them or their persona? It would feel disproportionate to speak of a female gaze, since pop music's principally patriarchal point of departure is rarely called into question (men experience things, women and other men adore them) but there is at least a possibility – exploited by female, queer and trans performers for a long time now and with increasing frequency – of escaping authenticism, of offering up a different trace of the body. The live-performance body and the media-transmitted body can never be interpreted without reference to its other physical state (or states). The fact that we always recognize a media-famous performer (or someone resembling them) in live settings, and that we always come close to real-world causes in purely media-based situations – and that this duality is reflected in the dual relations between self and persona, narrative and presence – is a challenge to pop music, daring it to enact its tradition of brokenness, of real-world causes and mediality in powerful tension, and to strengthen its fundamentally queer constellation of transgression at the expense of its other tendency towards vitality marketing and authenticism. Pop music's impossible and simultaneously ubiquitous physicality is and will remain its unique energy; it never belongs to a determinant subject, and may never submit to a determinant discourse or a determinant economy.

Notes

Chapter 1: Pop Music Is a Form of Indexical Art

1 'The gramophone listener actually wishes to listen to himself, and the artist simply offers him a substitute for the sounding image of his own person, which he would like to keep as a possession. The sole reason why he values the record is because he himself can be just as well preserved. Most of the time records are virtual photographs of their owners, flattering ones: ideologies.' Theodor W. Adorno, 'Nadelkurven' [The Curves of the Needle] (1927), in *Gesammelte Schriften* 19, Musikalische Schriften VI (Frankfurt am Main: Suhrkamp, 1984) pp. 525–529.

2 For the sake of argument, I shall borrow the famous triad from Charles Sanders Peirce's semiotic theory in more or less unaltered form: 'index' refers to content that causes the sign itself, 'icon' to content that resembles the sign, 'symbol' to conventional, agreed and

accepted, but otherwise arbitrary, content. In film and photographic theory, especially that of Gilles Deleuze, this theoretical structure is applied in augmented form, but this is too far-reaching for our purposes.

3 One might contend that the effects of such causes are also subject to the laws of nature. But, unlike the experiences of nature that produce effects called sublime in classical aesthetics, recordings are stationary, readily available for human enjoyment, and pose no threat to it, as – at least in the latter instance – the experience of nature on its own terms does.

4 Early media theory texts, and even later ones acknowledging the indexicality of recording, focus on other effects. Walter Benjamin's 1930s essay on the 'aura' – that which is lost by reproduction – overlooks the new type of aura that is acquired by chance through recording; see his *The Work of Art in the Age of Mechanical Reproduction* (London: Penguin, 2008). As early as 1928, Paul Valéry's 'The Conquest of Ubiquity', in *Aesthetics* (London: Routledge & Kegan Paul, 1964), identifies another aspect of recording and reproducibility that is relevant and interesting for our purposes: a new 'ubiquity' of the arts, and especially of music. In the 1970s, Rosalind Krauss's 'Notes on the Index', *October*, 3 (1977), pp. 68–81, confines its scope to contemporary visual art, specifically to what she calls 'thereness' – meaning not the indexicality embedded in symbolic and iconic phenomena in pop music and film, but the precise opposite of typical pop music (only in its most extreme formats [noise] does pop music ever share this trait with visual art). It was not until around

1980 that Roland Barthes's *Camera Lucida* outlined the phenomenological characteristic of indexical reception embedded in an invariably iconic photograph, coining it the 'punctum'; but he differentiates this concept in no uncertain terms from an aesthetic experience: the punctum cannot be intended, and is therefore a dimension of art unrelated to production aesthetics. Pop music depends on this gain in the practical dimension of punctum appreciation.

5 Béla Balázs, 'Visible Man' and 'The Spirit of Film', in Erica Carter (ed.), *Béla Balázs: Early Film Theory* (New York: Berghahn, 2010); Rudolf Arnheim, *Die Seele in der Silberschicht [The Soul in the Silver Layer]* (Frankfurt am Main: Suhrkamp, 2004); id., *The Film as Art* (Berkeley: University of California Press, 1957).

6 Georges Bataille, *Visions of Excess: Selected Writings 1927–1939* (Minneapolis: University of Minnesota Press, 1985).

7 Georges Didi-Huberman, *La ressemblance informe, ou Le gai savoir visuel selon Georges Bataaille [Formless Resemblance: or the Merry Visual Science According to Georges Bataille]* (Paris: Macula, 1995), especially the penultimate chapter.

8 Tom Gunning, 'The Cinema of Attractions', in Thomas Elsaesser, *Early Cinema: Space, Frame, Narrative* (London: British Film Institute, 2019).

9 Sergei Eisenstein, 'Montage of Attractions' (1923), in id., *Beyond the Shot*. 'An attraction is every aggressive moment . . . of course, in the sense of immediate reality, within which the Guignol theatre operates: gouging out eyes or cutting off hands and feet on stage.'

10 Callie Angell, *Andy Warhol Screen Tests* (New York: Abrams, 2006).

11 Various, *Music!* The Berlin Phonogram Archive, WERGO, 2000.

12 Mike Kelley and Scanner, *Esprits de Paris*, CD, Compound Annex, and Mike Kelley, 'An Academic Cut-Up, in Easily Digestible Paragraph-Size Chunks; Or, the New King of Pop: Dr Konstantin Raudive', in *Grey Room* 11 (New York: MIT, 2003), pp. 22–43.

13 Bruno Latour, *Reassembling the Social: An Introduction to Actor-Network Theory* (Oxford: Oxford University Press, 2005).

14 Karen Barad, *Meeting the Universe Halfway* (Durham, NC: Duke University Press, 2007).

15 Quentin Meillassoux, *After Finitude* (London: Continuum, 2008).

16 Even Adorno once wondered whether cheap, artless B-pictures were perhaps superior to A-list films, though he later rejected the idea after it gained traction. See Theodor W. Adorno, 'Filmtransparente' [Transparencies on Film], in *Ohne Leitbild – Parva Aesthetica*, Gesammelte Schriften Band 10.1, Kulturkritik und Gesellschaft I (Frankfurt am Main: Suhrkamp, 2003).

17 Jack Smith, 'The Perfect Filmic Appositeness of Maria Montez', in Ed Leffingwell (ed.), *Wait for Me at the Bottom of the Pool: The Writings of Jack Smith* (New York: Serpent's Tail, 1997).

18 Niklas Luhmann, *Art as a Social System* (Stanford: Stanford University Press, 2000), pp. 102–132.

Chapter 2: Pop Music Belongs to the Second of Three Culture Industries

1 As previously mentioned, I also refer to German media theory in the tradition of Friedrich Kittler.

2 Wolfgang Hagen, *Gegenwartsvergessenheit – Lazarsfeld, Adorno, Innis, Luhmann [Forgetting the Present: Lazarsfeld, Adorno, Innis, Luhmann]* (Berlin: Merve, 2003), pp. 43–64.

3 Friedrich Kittler, 'Copyright 1944 by Social Studies Inc.', in Sigrid Weigel (ed.), *Flaschenpost und Postkarte. Korrespondenzen zwischen Kritischer Theorie und Poststrukturalismus [Bottle Messages and Postcards: Correspondence Between Critical Theory and Post-structuralism]*, (Cologne/Weimar/Vienna: Böhlau, 1995, pp. 185–93).

Chapter 4: An Assembly of Effects and Small Noises

1 See for example Paul E. Willis, *Profane Culture* (London: Routledge, 1978), or Dick Hebdige, *Subculture: The Meaning of Styles* (London: Routledge, 1979).

2 Even in the Beatles' heyday in the mid-1960s, it was often the song, the composition itself, that defined success. In many countries, 'Michelle' first landed in the charts in a version by a forgotten band called The Overlanders and another by a duo called David and Jonathan; the Beatles' version arrived later. Teenagers and twentysomethings, who were familiar with the transcendent meaning of particular voices and of

specific bodies and sound effects, were not alone in the world; once the Beatles rose into the mainstream, they could also begin selling their songs to a differently socialized older generation.

3 Henry Flynt and George Maciunas, *Communists Must Give Revolutionary Leadership in Culture* (New York: World View Publishers, 1965).

4 Jacques Attali, *Noise: The Political Economy of Music* (Minneapolis: University of Minnesota Press, 1985).

5 A notable example here is the queer culture of opera diva worship that Wayne Koestenbaum discusses in *The Queen's Throat: Opera, Homosexuality and the Mystery of Desire* (New York: Poseidon, 1993).

6 This gives some people hope that through the methods of radical Japanese and American noise artists such as Merzbow or Hanatarash, 'spectacle' can be tackled head-on and brought down. See Csaba Toth, 'Noise Theory', in Xabier Erkizia, Mattin and Anthony Iles (eds.), *Noise & Capitalism* (Donostia/San Sebastian: Gipuzkoako Foru Aldundia – Arteleku, 2008).

7 Erving Goffman, *The Presentation of Self in Everyday Life* (Doubleday: New York, 1959).

8 In Eddie Cochran's 'Summertime Blues' (1958, later covered by T. Rex and The Who, among others), a young man complains, among other things, that his father won't lend him his car. He eventually reports this to his congressman, who responds: 'I'd like to help you son, but you're too young to vote.'

9 'Come mothers and fathers throughout the land / Don't criticize what you can't understand / Your sons and your daughters are beyond your command / Your

old world is rapidly fading' – from 'The Times They Are A-Changing.'

10 Henry Flynt, 'Concept Art', in LaMonte Young and Jackson MacLow (eds.), *An Anthology of Chance Operations* (Heiner Friedrich: New York, 1963).

Chapter 5: Minus Music: Popularity and Criticism

1 One widespread misunderstanding attributes this trait of pop music to 'official' individualism, within a culture of competition built upon profiteering from individual distinctiveness. But note that being alone is usually a hardship, not a position of strength. The fact that successful integration can take a distinction-alist course is undeniable, but is just one of several possibilities.

2 I am speaking of pop music only in the emphatic sense. By this I mean (beyond the above examples) all engagement with pop music that is perceived as exis-tentially important by its respective reception culture and that has significant influence on its self-image. Simple decorative or convention-bound background music (which in principle all pop music can become) and art (for pop music can easily become that too) are the polar extremes of this understanding of pop music.

Chapter 6: Production Aesthetics

1 Roland Barthes, *Camera Lucida* (New York: Hill and Wang, 1981), esp. pp. 42 ff.

2 For Barthes, 'studium' is the opposite of 'punctum'. It

means the intended, planned, deliberate elements of a photograph.

3 Barthes, *Camera Lucida*, p. 47.
4 See Jean-Jacques Nattiez, *The Boulez-Cage Correspondence* (Cambridge: Cambridge University Press, 1993).
5 See Helmut Salzinger, *Rock Power* (Reinbek bei Hamburg: Rowohlt, 1973).
6 Philip Core, *Camp: The Lie That Tells the Truth* (New York: Delilah, 1994).
7 Eve Kosofsky Sedgwick, *Epistemology of the Closet* (Berkeley: University of California Press, 1990), p. 156.
8 Craig Owens, 'Posing', in Craig Owens and Scott Bryson, *Beyond Recognition: Representation, Power and Culture* (Berkeley: University of California Press, 1992), pp. 201–217.
9 Roland Barthes, *The Neutral* (New York: Columbia University Press, 2005), pp. 21–28.
10 Here, I am of course employing the historical sense of this word, as developed in the beat generation literature of Norman Mailer and others, and repeatedly renewed thereafter. Nowadays, 'hipster' is usually a pejorative term depicting a very specific caricature of this character; this concept is not helpful in this structural and fundamentally non-judgemental analysis. Similarly, the appreciation in value of the 'nerd' in recent times is not accounted for here.
11 Pierre Bourdieu, 'Reconversion Strategies', in id., *Distinction: A Social Critique of the Judgement of Taste* (Cambridge, MA: Harvard University Press, 1984), pp. 125–168.